EYEWITNESS
ROCKS &
MINERALS

Slice from septarian nodule

Garnet-chlorite schist

Gypsum desert rose

Cinnabar

Hematite

Granite

Wenlock limestone with triolobite fossils

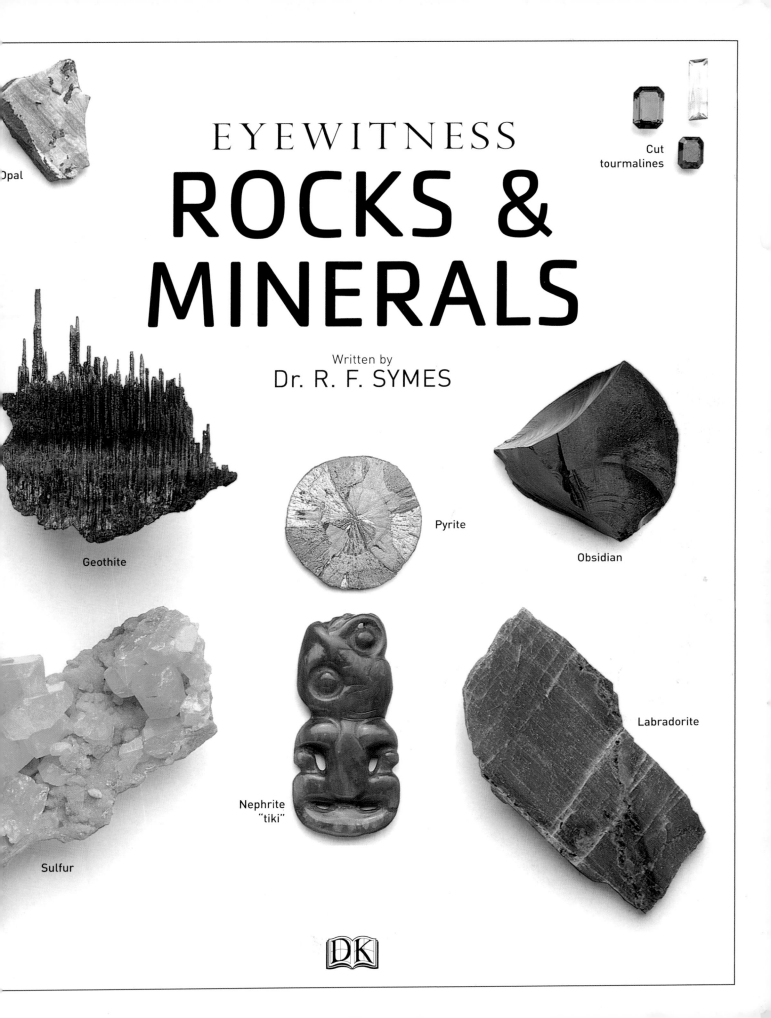

Opal

Cut
tourmalines

EYEWITNESS
ROCKS &
MINERALS

Written by
Dr. R. F. SYMES

Geothite

Pyrite

Obsidian

Sulfur

Nephrite
"tiki"

Labradorite

DK

Magnifying lens

DK

LONDON, NEW YORK,
MELBOURNE, MUNICH, AND DELHI

Project editor Janice Lacock
Art editor Neville Graham
Managing art editor Jane Owen
Special photography Colin Keates (Natual History
Museum, London) and Andreas Einsiedel
Editorial consultants Dr. R. F. Symes (Natural History Museum, London)
and Dr. Wendy Kirk (University College London)

RELAUNCH EDITION (DK UK)
Editor Ashwin Khurana
US editor Margaret Parrish
Senior designers Rachael Grady, Spencer Holbrook
Managing editor Gareth Jones
Managing art editor Philip Letsu
Publisher Andrew Macintyre
Producer, preproduction Adam Stoneham
Senior producer Charlotte Cade
Jacket editor Maud Whatley
Jacket designer Laura Brim
Jacket design development manager Sophia MTT
Publishing director Jonathan Metcalf
Associate publishing director Liz Wheeler
Art director Phil Ormerod

RELAUNCH EDITION (DK India)
Senior editor Neha Gupta
Art editor Deep Shikha Walia
Senior DTP designer Harish Aggarwal
DTP designers Anita Yadav, Pawan Kumar
Managing editor Alka Thakur Hazarika
Managing art editor Romi Chakraborty
CTS manager Balwant Singh
Jacket editorial manager Saloni Talwar
Jacket designers Govind Mittal, Suhita Dharamjit, Vidit Vashisht

First American Edition, 1988
This American Edition, 2014
Published in the United States by DK Publishing
4th floor, 345 Hudson Street
New York, New York 10014

14 15 16 17 18 10 9 8 7 6 5 4 3 2 1
196434—07/14

ISBN 978-1-4654-2056-5 (Paperback)
ISBN 978-1-4654- 2098-5 (ALB)

DK books are available at special discounts when purchased in bulk for sales
promotions, premiums, fund-raising, or educational use. For details, contact:
DK Publishing Special Markets, 345 Hudson Street, New York, New York 10014
or SpecialSale@dk.com.

Color reproduction by Alta Image Ltd., London, UK
Printed and bound by South China Printing Co. Ltd., China

Discover more at

www.dk.com

Chalcedony cameo

Mixed rough
and polished
pebbles

Chisel

Geologist's hammer

Contents

Cut citrine

Baryte desert rose

Clear topaz

Cut amethyst

Earth

One of eight planets that revolve around the Sun, Earth is thought to be about 4.6 billion years old. The word geology comes from the ancient Greek for Earth and study. The many different types of rocks found on our planet hold valuable details about Earth's long history, so geologists study them and figure out the processes and events that produced them.

Early view of Earth with a central fire

Earth's structure

Earth consists of a core, mantle, and crust. The crust and upper mantle form vast plates that move slowly over the mantle beneath. The closer to the Earth's center, the greater the temperature and pressure.

Crust, 4–43 miles (6–70 km) thick

Solid mantle, about 1,800 miles (2,300 km) thick

Molten outer core, about 1,400 miles (2,300 km) radius

Solid inner core, about 750 miles (1,200 km) radius

Basaltic magma from the mantle

Continental plate

Oceanic plate

Oceanic ridge

Volcanic range

Moving plates

Where plates collide, mountain ranges may form. Where they pull apart, magma rises to form deep-sea ridges. When one sinks beneath another, volcanoes erupt.

Precious metals
Platinum, silver, and gold are valuable, rare metals.

Seashore pebbles
These are formed by the weathering of larger rocks by wave action.

Gold in quartz vein

Crystal habits
The shape of a crystal is known as its habit.

Cubes of pyrite

Mineral ores
These are the source of most useful metals.

Cut citrine, a variety of quartz

Cassiterite, tin ore, from Bolivia

Diamond in kimberlite

Gemstones
Rare, hard-wearing, and attractive minerals may be cut as gemstones, mainly for jewelry.

Quartz crystals from France

Crystals
Many minerals form regular-shaped solids with flat surfaces, known as crystals.

Shell limestone

Fossils
These rocks contain the remains of, or impressions made by, former plants or animals.

Quartzite beach pebbles

Igneous rocks
The most common types of rock have formed from molten magma.

Granite

Nile Delta
Suez Canal
City of Cairo
Nile River

Satellite image of Nile River
Egypt's Nile River carries debris eroded from rocks and deposits it in the delta and sea, where it may slowly form sedimentary rocks.

Volcanic rocks
Volcanic activity produces a number of different types of rock and lava.

Hawaiian ropy lava

Lake Amboseli, a dry lake

Ingito Hills on edge of East African Rift Valley

Chyulu mountain range, Kenya

Carboniferous limestone

Sedimentary rocks
These rocks are formed by the accumulation and compaction of loose sediments that have built up in layers.

Anthracite, the hardest form of coal

Coal
One type of sedimentary rock, coal has formed from the fossilized remains of prehistoric plants.

Mount Meru
Mount Kilimanjaro
Pangani River valley
Glaciers of Kibo

Landsat image of East Africa
This area shows a range of landscapes, formed from different rocks, such as volcanic rocks forming volcanic Mount Kilimanjaro, and evaporites in dried-up lakes.

Rocks and their minerals

James Hutton (1726– 1797), one of the founders of modern geology

Rocks are natural aggregates or combinations of one or more minerals. Some rocks contain only one mineral, but most consist of more. Minerals are inorganic solids with definite chemical compositions and an ordered atomic arrangement. Here, two common rocks—granite and basalt—are shown with specimens of the major minerals of which they are formed.

Granite and its major minerals

Minerals' size and texture vary with how a rock forms. In the coarse-grained rock, granite, the major minerals are visible to the naked eye: quartz (1); mica (2); feldspar (3).

Quartz

Mica

Feldspar

Basalt and its major minerals

The main minerals in basalt are olivine (1), plagioclase feldspar (2), and pyroxene (3). Since it is fine-grained, it is not always possible to distinguish them with the naked eye. This olivine basalt was collected from a volcano in Hawaii.

Etched face

1 Olivine
Transparent green crystals of olivine are very rare and known as peridot.

2 Feldspa
Flat or polished crystal of labradorite (a plagioclase feldspar) displa beautiful colo

Iridescen blue and orange visible on the surfa

Augite crystal

1 Quartz
These quartz crystals have milky, etched faces.

3 Feldspar
Crystals of orthoclase (a feldspar) are pale pink or milky white.

3 Pyroxene
This well developed, single black crystal of augite (a pyroxene) comes from Italy. Augite crystals are found in various igneous rocks.

Rock matrix

2 Mica
Black biotite (a form of mica) crystals can be split into thin sheets.

Diverse forms

Rocks are not always hard and resistant—loose sand and wet clay are considered to be rocks. The individual size of minerals in a rock ranges from small specks, in a fine-grained volcanic rock, to many yards in a granite pegmatite.

Rocks formed within rocks

This sedimentary rock specimen is a claystone septarian nodule. Nodules such as this form when groundwater redistributes minerals within a rock in a particular nodular pattern. Here, the pattern of veins is formed of calcite.

Crystals of ore mineral

Orange-red tabular crystals of sulfenite form in lead- and molybdenum-bearing ore veins.

Eruption of Mount Pelée, Martinique, on August 5, 1851

Rocks from volcanic eruption

"Pele's hair" consists of golden-brown, hairlike fibers of basalt glass, which occasionally enclose minute olivine crystals. It was formed from the eruption of basaltic magma as a lava spray.

Rocks formed by evaporation

Stalactites are substances deposited when dripping water evaporates. This blue-green stalactite of the mineral chalcanthite (copper sulfate) was formed from percolating copper-rich waters in a mine.

Section of a mine roof colored with deposits of the copper mineral, chalcanthite

Lighter bands of pyroxene and plagioclase feldspar

Dark layer of chromite

Rocks that form in layers

Norite is an igneous rock made of the minerals pyroxene, plagioclase feldspar, and chromite. In this specimen, the dark and light minerals have separated into layers. The dark chromite layers constitute an important source of chromium.

How rocks are formed

Geological processes work in continual cycles, redistributing chemical elements, minerals, and rocks. These processes are driven by the Earth's internal heat and, at its surface, by the Sun's energy.

Andesite formed from a volcanic eruption in the Solomon Islands in the Pacific

Pure quartz sand formed from weathered granites o sandstone

Volcanic activity
When rocks of the crust and upper mantle melt, they form magma, which volcanic activity brings to Earth's surface as extrusive igneous rocks. Basalt is the most common.

Basaltic lava from Hawaii

Survivor
Le Puy de Dôme, France, is the plug once at the core of an ancient volcano.

Igneous inselberg
Sugar Loaf Mountain, Brazil, consists of intrusive igneous rocks exposed by weathering.

Volcanic activity

Weatheri

Surface

Igneous rocks

Melting

Magn

Migmatite from Finland

Gabbro, a basalt, from Finland

Feldspar crystal

Granite containing feldspar crystals, from England

Melting
Occasionally, high temperatures and pressures cause rocks to melt partially. If the rock is then squeezed, snaking veins may form. Migmatites are mixed rocks with a metamorphic host, such as gneiss or schist, cut by veins of granite.

Rocks from magma
Rocks formed within Earth from molten magma are called intrusive igneous rocks. Those that cooled slowly, deep under the surface (such as granite), are called plutonic, after Pluto, the Greek god of the underworld.

Weathering

[A]s wind, rain, ice, and heat act on rocks, [th]ey may may lead to chemical changes [or] cause the rocks to fragment and form [s]ediments, such as sand grains and clays.

Clays produced by weathering become important components of soils

Deposition of sediments

Sediments are transported by rivers, or by the wind in desert regions, and eventually deposited into layers of different-sized particles. When compacted, the layers form sedimentary rocks.

Layered sandstone from the US

River transportation

Rivers such as these (seen from space) transport rock debris from one area to another. Each day, the Mississippi deposits thousands of tons of debris into its delta.

Banded claystone from Uganda

The rock cycle

[T]here is no starting point [in] this cycle, which has been [go]ing on for millions of years.

Transport

Deposition

Heat and pressure

Sedimentary rocks

[M]etamorphic [ro]cks

Desert sandstone from Scotland that is 200-million-year-old

Metamorphic rocks

Quartz veins stand out in this schist rock face in Scotland, an area that is rich in metamorphic rocks.

Quartzite, an altered sandstone, formed by pressure and heat

Gneiss, a banded metamorphic rock

Granite

Gneiss

Mica schist formed from metamorphosed claystones

Metamorphism

The deeper a rock is within Earth, the greater the pressure exerted on it from the overlying rocks, and the higher the temperature. Pressure and heat cause the rocks to change or "metamorphose" as the minerals recrystallize. The new rocks (such as gneiss, mica, and quartzite, above) are termed metamorphic rocks.

Weathering and erosion

Rocks at the Earth's surface all break down. Weathering, chemical or mechanical, breaks them down as they stand. Erosion breaks them down further as they are moved, by the action of water, ice, or wind.

Wind erosion

Sediment-laden wind may slowly grind away at a rock.

Monument Valley, US
Abrasion by the wind produces large, protruding "buttes."

Abrasion by the wind
Softer layers of rock are worn away, leaving the harder ones protruding.

Sand blasting
Faceted sand-blown desert pebbles are called "dreikanters."

Weathering caused by temperature

The expansion and contraction of rock as the temperature varies causes it to break up. Water expanding in the rock as it freezes can cause frost-shattering.

Sandstone composed of sand accumulated 200 million years ago in a desert environment

Sand from a present-day desert in Saudi Arabia

Desert erosion
In deserts, where sediment is carried by wind, rocks are often reddish and composed of rounded sand grains.

Desert environment
Wind and temperature changes cause continual weathering and barren landscapes in the Sahara Desert.

Onion-skin weathering
Changes in temperature cause the surface layers of rock to expand, contract, and peel away.

Fine-graine doleri

Onion-sk weather doleri

Peeling layer like onion skin expose the underlying rock

Chemical weathering

Minerals dissolved by acidic rainwater at the surface may be carried down into the soil and rock below.

Fresh, unaltered granite (left)

Altered minerals
Granite is split as water freezes and expands. Its chemically altered minerals form coarse rock.

Rock altered by percolating groundwater

Secondary minerals

Coarse, weathered granite

Chemical changes
These brightly colored "secondary minerals" were formed from deposits of dissolved minerals from weathered rocks higher up.

Granite tors, UK
Tors are weathered, rounded rocks left when surrounding rock has been eroded away.

Tropical weathering
In the tropics, quartz is dissolved and carried off, while feldspars are altered to clay minerals that may form a surface deposit of bauxite.

Ice erosion
As glaciers move they pick up fragments of rock, which form part of its icy base. The moving, frozen mass causes further erosion of underlying rocks.

Large rock fragment

Scratches caused by a glacier

Parthenon, Athens, Greece
Chemicals in the air can react with stone and cause weathering of monuments.

Swiss glacier
Glaciers are a major cause of erosion in mountainous regions.

Scratched rock
This limestone from Grindelwald, Switzerland, was gouged by fragments of rock in the glacier that flowed over it.

Glacier deposits
A till is a deposit left by a melting glacier and contains crushed rock fragments. Ancient tills formed into hard rock are called "tillite." This specimen is from the Flinders Ranges in South Australia, which was glaciated some 600 million years ago.

Rocks on the seashore

Many seashores are backed by cliffs. Coarse material that has fallen from above is gradually broken up by the sea and sorted into pebbles, gravel, sand, and mud. These various sizes are then deposited separately—the raw material for future sedimentary rocks.

Pebbles on Chesil Beach, England

Graded grains
On the beach, these pebbles are sorted by waves and tides. The sand is pure quartz—other minerals were washed away.

Large, coarse pebbles

Irregularly shaped pyrite nodule

Skimming stones
The best skimming stones are disk-shaped and are probably sedimentary or metamorphic rocks, as they split into sheets.

Mica schist

Slates

Hidden crystals
Pyrite nodules are common in chalk areas. The dull, bumby outside breaks open to reveal glistening crystals inside.

Local stones
These pebbles are metamorphic rocks that have been worn into flat disks on the beach where they were collected.

Shell pebbles
Uninhabited sea shells are battered by continuous wave action. In time, the fragments are smoothed into pebbles, like these ones from a beach in New Zealand.

Amber pebbles
Amber is the fossil resin of extinct coniferous trees that lived thousands of years ago. It is especially common along the Baltic coasts of Russia and Poland.

Preserved waves
Visible at low tide, ripple marks form under water from sand carried by currents. This Finnish specimen preserves long-ago ripple marks in sandstone.

lacks sands

areas of volcanic activity,
each sand may be rich in dark
minerals. The olivine sand comes
from Scotland; the magnetite-
bearing sand is from Tenerife.

Dark olivine sand

Magnetite-bearing sand

Black volcanic ash beach on north
coast of Santorini, Greece

Medium-sized, coarse pebbles

Small, fine pebbles

Finest pebbles

Quartz sand

Found in chalk
Because flint nodules
are hard, they resist
abrasion and may be
seen on beaches in
chalk areas (right).

White Cliffs of Dover, UK

*Marcasite
nodule, split
in two*

*Marcasite interior
reveals crystals
radiating outward*

Granitic origin
In granite country,
beach pebbles tend
to be of quartz,
an abundant vein
mineral, or pink
or gray granite.

Foreign material
Not all beach
rocks are of
local derivation.
This porphyritic
igneous rock
was probably
carried across
the North Sea
from Norway to
England by ice
during the last
Ice Age.

Flint nodules from below chalk cliffs

Assorted glass pebbles

Brick pebble

Synthetic pebbles
Man-made objects may be washed ashore or dumped
on the beach. Some of them may eventually become
abraded and rounded by wave action.

Protecting the beach
Artificial groynes stop
sand drifting.

15

Igneous rock

These rocks form when magma from deep within Earth's crust and upper mantle cools and solidifies. Intrusive ones solidify within the crust and are later exposed by erosion; extrusive ones form when magma erupts as lava and cools.

Basalt needle, St. Helena

Giant's Causeway
When basaltic lava cools, it often forms hexagonal columns, as in Northern Ireland

Biotite granite

Graphic granite

Red granite

Black grains are biotite, a form of mica

Long, angular quartz crystals look like ancient writing against the larger, pale-pink feldspar crystals

Red coloring due to the high proportion of potassium feldspar in the rock

Granite
An extemely common intrusive rock, granite consists mainly of coarse grains of quartz, feldspar, and mica. The grains are large because they formed as the molten magma cooled slowly deep in the Earth. Generally mottled, granite varies from gray to red according to the different proportions of constituent minerals.

Pitchstone
Formed when volcanic lava cools very quickly, pitchstone contains some crystals of feldspar and quartz, but it has a dull, resinlike appearance and may be brown, black, or gray.

Obsidian
Like pitchstone, obsidian is a glass formed from rapidly cooled lava. It forms so quickly there is no time for crystals to grow. Its characteristically sharp edges made it useful as an early tool.

Feldspar porphyry
Porphyries are rocks that contain large crystals called "phenocrysts" within a medium-grained rock. This particular sample contains feldspar crystals and comes from Wales.

Phenocryst of feldspar

Olivine

Pyroxene

Plagioclase feldspar

Gabbro
An intrusive rock, gabbro consists of dark minerals such as olivine and augite. It has coarse grains as large crystals formed when the magma slowly cooled.

Thin section of gabbro
When a thin slice of rock is seen under a microscope using a certain kind of light, hidden features, such as the crystal shapes of its minerals, appear.

Vesicular basalt

Empty vesicles or holes

Basalt
Formed from solidified lava, basalt is the most common extrusive rock. It is similar in composition to gabbro but finer grained. When the lava cools, it may split into many-sided columns, as seen at St. Helena's Needle and Northern Ireland's Giant's Causeway.

Amygdaloidal basalt

Hole filled with calcite

Vesicular volcanic rocks
These two rocks from the volcanically active islands of Hawaii are basalts that were formed when bubbles of gas were trapped in hot lava scum. The vesicular basalt is light and full of holes known as "vesicles." In amygdaloidal basalt, the holes were later filled in with minerals such as calcite.

Peridotite
A dark, heavy rock mainly containing the minerals olivine and pyroxene, peridotite is thought to underlie layers of gabbro 6 miles (10 km) beneath the ocean floor.

Green olivine crystals

Dark pyroxene crystals

Calcite vein

Serpentinite
This coarse-grained, red-and-green rock is named after its dominant mineral, serpentine. It is streaked with white veins of calcite. Serpentinite is common in the Alps.

Volcanic rock

Rocks formed by volcanic activity can be divided into pyroclastic rocks and acid and basic lavas. The first are formed from either solid rock fragments o "bombs" of lava that solidify as they fly through the air. Acid lavas are thick, sticky, and flow very slowly forming steep-sided volcanoes. The more fluid, fast-flowing basic lavas spread over vast areas.

Ejection of lava from Eldfell, Iceland, 1973

Pyroclastic rocks

Pyroclastic rocks consist of rock and lava pieces that were blown apart by exploding gases.

Agglomerate formed close to a vent

Volcanic bombs

When blobs of lava are thrown out of a volcano, some solidify in the air and land on the ground as hard "bombs." These two specimens are shaped like footballs, but bombs may be spherical or irregular in appearance.

Intrusion breccia formed within a vent

Mixed-up pieces

The force of an explosion may cause rocks to fragment. The angular pieces land inside or close to the vent and form rocks known as agglomerates

Ash

Inside a volcano

Magma flows through a central vent or side vents. It may form underground dykes that cut across rock layers or sills parallel to them.

Vent

Side vent

Magma

Sill

Dyke

Bedded tuff (a hardened ash)

Wind-blown particles

Volcanic ash can travel thousands of miles in the atmosphere. Where it settles and hardens it forms tuff. When Mount St. Helens erupted in 1980, coarse grains were blown 3 miles (5 km); the wind carried fine particles 17 miles (27 km).

Eruption of Mount St. Helens, Washington, 1980

esuvius, 79 CE
his famous eruption produced a
uée ardente, a fast-moving cloud
 magma and ash, and destroyed
e Roman town of Pompeii.

Aphthitalite

hthitalite

ocks from gases
active volcanoes are "dormant"
t volcanic gases may escape
d hot springs form, with
inerals forming rocks like
is one from Vesuvius.

inoan ruins, Santorini
e island blew apart c. 1450 BCE.

Acid lavas

These sticky lavas may solidify in the volcano's vent, trap gases, then explode.

Floating rocks
Pumice is solidified
lava froth. Because the
froth contains bubbles
of gas, the rock is
peppered with holes.
Pumice is the only rock
that floats in water.

Natural glass
Although chemically the
same as pumice, obsidian has
a totally different, glassy
texture. Because it has sharp
edges, obsidian was used by
primitive man to make tools,
arrowheads, and ornaments.

Molasseslike lavas
This light-colored, fine-grained
rock is called rhyolite. The
distinctive bands formed as the
sticky, viscous lava flowed for
short distances.

Basic lavas

These lavas flow smoothly, forming flatter volcanoes or welling up through cracks
in the ocean floor. As a result, the vent does not get choked and gases can escape,
so that although there is plenty of lava, few pyroclastic rocks are formed.

Runny lavas
Basaltic lavas are fast-flowing
and quickly spread to cover
vast areas. This specimen of
basalt was deposited by the
Hualalai volcano on Hawaii.

**Ropy
lava**
As lava flows,
the surface cools
and forms a skin
that wrinkles as the
fluid center flows on.

**Colorful
crystals**
Sparkling points in
this basalt include green
olivine and black pyroxene crystals.

Sedimentary rock

Weathered and eroded rocks break into smaller pieces of rock and minerals. This sediment may be transported to a new site (often a lake, river, or sea) and deposited in layers that become buried and compacted. Cemented together, the particles form new, sedimentary rocks.

Thin section of limestone

Under the microscope, ammonite shells show up against the mud that buried them. Ammonites are now extinct—this rock is about 160 million years old.

Ammonite shell

Mud backgrou

Fossilized shells embedded in rock

Chalk

Oolitic limeston

Rock builders

Rarely bigger than a pinhead, foraminifera are marine organisms that secrete lime. When they die, the shells fall to the ocean floor, where they eventually become cemented into limestone.

Shell limestone

Gastropod limestone

Remains of gastropod shell

Rounded grains known as "ooliths"

Flint

A form of silica, lumps of flint are often found in limestones, especially chalk. They are gray or black, but may be covered in a white, powderlike material. Like obsidian, when flint is broken, it has a "conchoidal" fracture (see p. 48).

Limestone

Many sedimentary rocks consist of the remains of once-livi organisms. In these shelly and gastropod limestones, the remains animals are clearly visible in the rock. Chalk is al a limestone, formed from the skeletons of tiny s animals too small to see with t naked eye. Oolite, anoth limestone, forms in t sea as calcite builds around grains of san As they are rolled and fro by waves, t grains become larg

Algal limestone

So-called "muddy" limestones, like this one bound together by algae, are often referred to as "landscape marbles"—when the minerals crystallize they may produce patterns in the shapes of trees and bushes.

ple-filled, irregularly shaped rock

alcareous tufa
n extraordinary looking evaporite,
is porous rock is formed by the
aporation of spring water and is
metimes found in limestone caves.

Gypsum crystals growing from a central point like daisy petals

Evaporites
Some sedimentary rocks
are formed when saline
waters (often seawater)
evaporate and leave
deposits of minerals.
Examples include
halite and gypsum.
Halite is better known
as rock salt, from
which we get table
salt. Gypsum is used
to make plaster of
Paris, and in its massive
form it is called alabaster.

Single crystals
of rock salt are
not found as
often as
massive
samples

Halite

Gypsum

Reddish cast caused by impurities in the salt

rand Canyon, US
is site is eroded red
ndstone and
nestone.

Grit

Red sandstone

Sandstones
Both these rocks are
made from grains of sand
cemented together.
The red sandstone
comes from a
desert where wind
rubbed and rounded
the quartz grains.
Grit is rougher—its
more angular grains
were buried before they
could be rubbed smooth.

Clay
Formed of microscopically fine
grains, clay feels sticky when wet.
When it is compacted and all the
water forced out of it, it forms hard
rocks called mudstone or shale.

edded volcanic ash
many sedimentary rocks, individual
ers of sediments form visible bands.
re, the stripes are layers of volcanic
h. The surface has been polished to
ghlight this feature.

Flint pebble

Conglomerate
The flint pebbles in this rock were
rounded by water as they rolled around
on river- or seabeds. After they were
buried, they became cemented together
to form a rock known as conglomerate.

Large rock fragment

Breccia
Like conglomerate, breccias contain
fragments of rock; however, these are
much more angular as they have not been
rounded by water or carried far from their
original home—often at the bottom of cliffs.

Limestone

Limestone caves, lined with dripping stalactites and giant stalagmites, are formed when slightly acidic rainwater turns the limestone's carbonate into bicarbonate, which is soluble in water and is carried away.

Top section attached to the roof of cave

Point of intersection

Stalactites of this thickness may take hundreds of years to form

Stalactites

Stalactites are formed in caves by groundwater containing dissolved lime dripping from the roof and leaving a deposit as it evaporates. Growing downward a fraction of an inch each year—shown in annual growth rings—they may slowly reach many feet in length.

Single stalactite formed from two smaller ones growing together

Swallow hole through which surface water flows underground

Limestone pavement consisting of large, jointed blocks

Underground lake   *Caves*

Limestone landscapes

Rainwater dissolves calcite in limestone, producing deep, narrow cracks ("grikes"). In time, the water enlarges them into passages. Flowing water dissolves the rock, producing "swallow holes" at the junctions between grikes. Underground streams form lakes in the caves.

Plan de Sales, France
Limestone pavements of flat blocks occur where weathering leaves no insoluble residue to make soil.

Tufa

A type of rock known as a precipitate, tufa forms when lime is deposited from water onto a rock surface in areas of low rainfall.

Coral-like structure

Ease Gill Caves, England
The forest of fine stalactites and stalagmites in this cave form the most spectacular part of a much larger, complex cave system under the hills of the Lancashire Pennines. In fact, this is the largest cave system in the UK.

Odd-shaped stalactite

Prominent growth rings mark the gradual development of the stalactite as successive deposits formed

Point onto which overhead drips fall

range twin talactite

Last section to grow

Stone Forest, China
The staggering landscape of the Hunan Province of China is typical of "karst" scenery. Named after the limestone area of Karst in Yugoslavia, the term is applied to many limestone regions, including the Cumberland Plateau, Tennessee, parts of the Blue Mountains, Australia, and the Causses, France.

Pamukkale Falls, Turkey
Beautiful travertine terraces are formed from the precipitation of calcite from hot springs in limestone areas. Travertine is quarried as a decorative building stone.

Stalagmites
Stalagmites are formed on the floor of caves where water has dripped from the roof or a stalactite above. As with stalactites, they develop as water containing dissolved lime evaporates.
  If stalactites and stalagmites grow together and join, forming pillars, they are often described as "organ pipes," "hanging curtains," and "portcullises."

End attached to floor of the cave

Color caused by impurities in the deposit

Layer of relatively pure calcite

Inside a stalactite
This specimen has been sliced through the center to reveal colored bands. The different colors show how the stalactite formed from deposits of lime with varying degrees of purity. The purest parts are the whitest.

Metamorphism

Metamorphic rocks are igneous or sedimentary rocks altered by heat and/or pressure. Such conditions can occur during the mountain-building process, as buried rocks are subjected to high temperatures and squeezed or folded, creating new minerals.

Schist

Thin section of garnet-mica schist
Seen through a petrological microscope, this rock reveals bright, blade-shaped mica crystals. Quartz and feldspar appear as shades of gray.

Marbles

When limestone is exposed to very high temperatures, new crystals of calcite grow and form the compact rock known as marble. This can look similar to the rock, quartzite, but marble is softer and easily scratched with a knife. Some medium-grained marble looks sugary or "saccharoidal." The marble far right was made from limestone containing impurites, such as pyroxene.

Saccharoidal marble

Evenly sized grains give a sugary appearance

Nodular gray marble

Pyroxene-bearing marble

Spotted hornfels

Chiastolite slate

Elongated chiastolite crystals

Aggregates of carbon

Spotted slate

From slate to hornfels

The irregular speckles in spotted slate are small aggregates of carbon, formed by heat from an igneous intrusion. In rocks nearer the intrusion, the temperature is considerably higher and needlelike crystals of chiastolite form in the slate. The rocks very close to the intrusion become so hot that they completely recrystallize and form a tough, new rock called hornfels.

Blue, bladelike crystals of kyanite

Red garnet crystals

Schists

Schist is formed from shale or mud but at a higher temperature than slate. The garnet-muscovite-chlorite schist was exposed to temperatures of at least 932°F (500°C). Kyanite-staurolite schist forms under high pressure, 6–9 miles (10–15 km) below ground.

Garnet-muscovite-chlorite schist

Kyanite-staurolite schist

19th-century slate quarry

late

uring mountain building, ale was squeezed so hard at its flaky micas crystallized right angles to the pressure. e resulting rock—slate— lits easily into thin sheets.

Light-colored layer containing quartz and feldspar

Dark band of biotite

Black biotite crystals

Blue kyanite crystals

Banded gneiss

Biotite-kyanite gneiss

Crystals of a green variety of pyroxene

Red garnet crystals

clogite

oduced under very high pressure, eclogite is tremely dense and is thought to form in the antle—far deeper than most other rocks. It ntains pyroxene and small, red crystals of garnet.

Gneisses

At high temperatures and pressures, sedimentary or igneous rocks may be metamorphosed to gneisses. These rocks have coarser grains than medium-grained schists and are easily identified because the minerals often separate into bands. These layers may be irregular where the rock has been folded under pressure.

Dark host rock

Migmatite

Under intense heat, parts of rocks may start to melt and flow, creating swirling patterns. This is very often shown in migmatites. They are not composed of one rock but are a mixture of a dark host rock with lighter-colored granitic rock. This sample is from the Scottish Highlands.

Pink granitic rock

Marble

Marble is a metamorphosed limestone, but its name is often used in the stone industry for a variety of other rocks. All are valued for their attractive range of textures and colors, and because they are easily cut and polished.

In the raw
A true marble, this unpolished, coarsely crystalline specimen of Mijas Marble is from Malaga, Spain. Polishing will give it a smooth surface.

Medici Madonna
Michelangelo sculpted this statue from Carrara marble, c. 1530.

Carrara quarry
The world's most famous marble comes from the Carrara quarry in Tuscany, Italy. It was the local stone for Michelangelo.

Greek connection
Originally from the Greek Island of Euboea, streaked Cipollino marble (above) is now quarried in Switzerland, the island of Elba, and Vermont.

Italian specialty
Gray Bardilla marble (left) comes from the Carrara quarry.

Italian elegance
Another striking Italian marble (right) is the black-and-gold variety from Liguria.

Tuscan stones

The distinctive texture of the Italian decorative stone, Breccia Violetto, was the reason for its use in the Paris Opera House in 1875.

Taj Mahal, India

This monument uses many marbles.

South African swirls

Polished travertine has beautiful swirling patterns. This piece is from Cape Province, South Africa.

Swiss origins

The limestone breccia known as Macchia-vecchia is quarried in Mendrisio, Switzerland.

Detail of marble inlay on the Taj Mahal

African copper

Quarried in Swaziland, Green Verdite's vivid coloring is caused by the presence of copper.

Algerian rock

Breche Sanguine or Red African (bottom) is a red breccia from Algeria. The Romans used it in the Pantheon, Rome, in the 1st century CE.

The first flint tools

Because flint splits in any direction, fractures to a sharp edge, and is fairly widespread, it was used in prehistoric times to make early tools and weapons.

Rough flint
nodule found
in chalk
areas

*Leather thong
securing flint and
antler sleeve to handle*

Tools from flint
Flint was shaped by detaching flakes from a nodule to leave a core that gradually became more refined.

Stone-on-stone
Striking the flint with a stone created sharp, jagged edges.

Pressure-flaking
Pointed implements such as antler bones gave tools sharper cutting edges.

Sharp-edged to
used for skinni

Scrapers we
used to dre
animal hid

Flint flakes
and chippings

Large, sharpened
hand ax

*Cutting
edge*

Light-
colored
hand ax

Small,
sharpened
hand ax

Crude
early
chopper

*Rough cutting
edge*

Ea
men usi
hand ax

Hand axes
Paleolithic hand axes were used to smash animal bones, skin hunted animals, and cut wood and plants. The well developed, dark axes are 70,000–300,000 years old. The lighter-colored ax dates from around 70,000–35,000 BCE.

Sharp cutting edge

Hafted adzes were used to hollow out canoes

Danish ax and dagger

The shape of this Early Bronze Age ax, found in the Thames River in the UK, shows it was imported. Polished with care, it was clearly an object of value. So, too, was the Early Bronze Age flint dagger (2,300–1,200 BCE), which imitates the shape of the earliest copper daggers.

Ax

Flint dagger

solithic
ze

Antler sleeve

Hafted adzes

Adzes have an asymmetrical cutting edge, with the blade at right angles to the handle. They were swung vertically to shape wood. These adzes date from the Mesolithic period (10,000–4,000 BCE).

Adze mounted directly onto handle

Asymmetrical cutting edge of flint

Arrowheads

The bow and arrow was invented in the Mesolithic period, and was still used for hunting in the Early Neolithic period, when leaf-shaped arrowheads were common. Later, in the Beaker period (2,750–1,800 BCE), barbed arrowheads were characteristic.

Neolithic arrowheads

Beaker arrowheads

Sickle

Flint sickles show crops were cultivated. The long, slightly curved blade was swung sideways to reap crops. A "gloss" on their cutting edge shows repeated harvesting. This one is Neolithic (4,000–2,300 BCE).

Reproduction wooden handle

Ninth-century obsidian ax from Mexico

Reproduction wooden handle

Flint daggers

Rare and made with care, these two daggers from the Beaker period were not just weapons, but status symbols, too.

Spearhead with obsidian blade from the Admiralty Islands, off Papua New Guinea

Obsidian

Like flint, obsidian was used in early tools because it fractures with sharp edges.

Rocks as tools

Archeologists have found numerous examples of other stone implements besides flint, from many different cultures around the world. Some were used as weapons or status symbols, others as agricultural or domestic tools.

Brazilian stone ax

Neolithic ax showing a highly polished surface

Neolithic ax made of diorite, an igneous rock

Neolithic ax made of rhyolitic tuff, a volcanic rock

Wedge to stop the stone from moving

Bored quartzite pebble

Stone axes

These stone axes date back to Neolithic Britain (4,000–2,300 BCE). Highly polished and tougher than flaked flint axes, they were traded over long distances—the source rocks were far from the places where the axes were found.

Digging stic[k]

During the Mesolithic a[nd] Neolithic periods (10,00[0–] 2,300 BCE), sticks weighted w[ith] pierced pebbles were used [to] break up the ground to pla[nt] crops or dig up roo[ts]

Breaking u[p] ground wit[h] a digging stick prior to planting

Battle axes

These perforated axes belong to the Early Bronze Age (2,300– 1,200 BCE) and are so well preserved that they could have been status symbols for display as well as for use as weapons. The bottom one was both an ax and a hammer.

Side view of battle ax made of diori[te]

Top view of battle ax

Reproduction wooden stick

Sharpened wooden point for digging hard ground

Carved stone maul (a war club or mace) made by Haida Indians, a North American tribe that lives on islands off British Columbia

Dual-purpose granite ax-hammer

Hammer end

Ax end

South African digging stick with horn point and stone weight

Whetstones

...onze implements
...ere sharpened by
...bbing the blunt edge
...ainst a whetstone.
...ese two are Bronze
...e (2,300–700 BCE) and
...re worn on a cord.

Engraved Viking forge stone made of soapstone and used in metalworking

A bird-shaped mortar carved by Haida Indians

Marble makeup palette

The Romans used powdered lead and chalk to whiten skin; red ocher to tint lips and cheeks; and soot to darken eyebrows. These were put on stone palettes, mixed with water or gum, and applied as a paint or paste.

Stone spindle whorl

To spin wool or cotton into thread, the Romans weighted a bone or wooden spindle with a stone whorl. The weight and rotating motion help twist the thread, which was then wound on to the spindle.

Roman rotary quern

...portable quern was used for grinding
...rn between two stones. The upper
...e was held in place by a spindle
...d was rotated by a handle. Grain
...s fed through the hole in the
...per stone, and the rotary
...tion forced it between
...e two grinding surfaces.

...ing a quern to grind
...rn during the Iron Age

Handle

Rotating stone

...ain
...ady
... grinding

Conglomerate lower stone (fixed to a bench or bedded in the ground)

31

Pigments

For body and rock art, early man crushed local rocks and mixed the powders with animal fats to produce a range of pigments. Over the centuries, as trading routes expanded, new colors were added to the artist's palette.

Brown clay

Powder brown cl

Earthy hue

Clays were widely us by early artists becau they were easy to sour and, being fine-graine easily pulverize

Green clay

Powdered green clay

Ocher paint

Umber paint

Shades of white

The first white pigment was chalk or, in some areas, kaolin (china clay) instead.

Powdered chalk

Color variation in a mineral

Many minerals are uniformly colored, but some come in a range of colors. For example, tourmaline (above) may occur as black, brown, pink, green, and blue crystals, or show a variety of colors in a single crystal.

Cave paintin

The earliest known artworks we made with a mixture of clays, chal earths, and burned wood and bone

Chalk White paint

Bison from Grotte de Niaux, France, c. 20,000 BCE

Color clues

A useful aid when identifying a mineral is the color that it produces when you crush it. Or simply scrape a sample across an unglazed white tile—many minerals leave a distinct, colored streak, which may or may not be the same color as the mineral; others have no discernible streak.

Orpiment

Cinnabar

Crocoite

Chalcopyrite

Hematite

Molybdenite

Powdered charcoal

Black as coal

Still popular with artists today, charcoal was well-known to cave painters— from the embers of their fires.

Lamp Black paint

Powdered
hematite

Powdered
realgar

kin coloring
e earthy variety of
matite, an iron ore,
oduces a rich reddish-brown
gment. Very finely powdered, it
s also used as makeup for skin.

Red paint

Arsenic
Orange paint

Egyptian
orange
About 1,500 BCE, Egyptians
first crushed realgar, an
arsenic compound found
in hot spring deposits, to
form an orange pigment.

Powdered
malachite

Powdered
orpiment

King's Yellow
paint

Malachite
Green
paint

Bright gold
Medieval
artists used
orpiment, an
arsenic compound,
to make many colors and
to imitate gold.

rilliant green
onze-Age Egypt first used
alachite, a copper compound, for green.

Powdered
lapis lazuli

Ultramarine
paint

Powdered
azurite

Powdered
cinnabar

Precious
blue
The refinement of
lapis lazuli powder
into a rich ultramarine
(and expensive) blue was first
achieved in Persia (now Iran).

Natural
vermilion
The bright,
vermilion red
of cinnabar
(mercuric
sulfide) was
used in
prehistoric China,
but only came into
widespread use in
the Middle Ages.

assical
ue
e copper
mpound
urite produced
ighly prized blue
ment that was widely
ed in classical antiquity.

Azurite
Blue paint

Vermilion
paint

Bright painting
By the late 13th
century, artists were
regularly using
ultramarine and
vermilion, as in
this painting
by Duccio.

Building stones

Most of the great monuments of the past survive because they were made from tough, natural stone. Today, natural building stones are mainly used for decoration, and man-made materials for construction.

Quarrying in the early 19th century was still done almost entirely by manual labor

Nummulitic limestone

Formed 40 million years ago, nummulite, a foraminiferan, is a famous limestone from the same quarries that supplied stone for the pyramids near Cairo, Egypt.

The pyramids, Egypt, made of local limestone

Fossils

Portland stone

After the Great Fire of London in 1666, St. Paul's Cathedral was rebuilt with this English limestone. The marks are made by "tooling," a decorative technique.

Tooling

Oolitic limestone

This building stone formed some 160 million years ago.

Welsh slate

Christian mosaic

Small fragments of local stones were often used for mosaic floors.

Limestone used for roofing

Slate

Unlike most building materials, roofing stones must split easily into thin sheets. Slate is ideal, but where it was not available, builders used local, often inferior, stone.

Notre Dame, Paris
This famous cathedral in Paris, France, was built from local limestone from the St. Jacques region of the city, between 1163 and 1250. The catacombs in Paris are old quarries.

Interlocking roof tile

Pantile

Sandstones
Various colored sandstones make excellent building stones, as seen in many fine Mogul monuments in India.

Man-made
Even man-made stone substitutes, such as brick and tiles, cement, concrete, and glass, originate from rocks of some kind.

Sandstone is 230 million years old

ranite
lished granite is often used the facades of buildings, in the imperial city of Petersburg, Russia.

Roofing tiles
In many parts of the world, man-made roofing tiles are made from clay.

Textured buff brick

Early skyscraper
New York's Empire State Building was made of mostly granite and sandstone but also some man-made materials.

Red sandstone from Scotland used as a cladding building stone

Smooth red brick

Great Wall of China
At 1,500 miles (2,400 km) long, the world's biggest construction uses various materials that change with the terrain it passes through. Parts include brick, granite, and many local rocks.

Bricks
Easily molded clays are fired to make bricks. Impurities in clays produce various colors and strengths.

Cement
Made by grinding and heating a limestone, cement mixed with sand, gravel, and water produces concrete.

The story of coal

The coal we burn is millions of years old. In the swampy forests of Asia, Europe, and North America, rotting leaves, seeds, and dead wood became buried. Overlying sediments squeezed out the water and compressed the plant matter into peat and then coal, layer upon layer. As pressure and heat grew, other types of coals were formed.

Plant roots

Fossilized wood
Jet is hard, black, but very light and is derived from driftwood laid down in the sea. Polished and carved, often for jewelry, it has been used since the Bronze Age.

Coal as jewelry
A major source of jet is Yorkshire, in northern England. These Roman pendants, found in York, were probably made of local jet.

Oil shale
A sedimentary rock, oil shale contains kerogen, an organic substance of plant and animal origin. When heated, kerogen gives off a vapor from which oil is extracted.

Leaf

Stalk

Seed case

The origins of coal
Carboniferous swamps may have looked similar to this stylized engraving.

The raw ingredients of coal
In areas with thick layers of vegetation and poor drainage, such as swamps or bogs, dead plants become waterlogged. They start to rot, but cannot decay completely.

The peat layer
Peat is a more compact form of the surface layer of rotting plants. Some roots and seed cases are still visible. Newly formed peat can be cut, dried, and burned as a fuel.

Cutting peat
This Irish turf-cutter is cutting peat by hand; machines can also be used.

Brown coal
Naturally compressed peat forms crumbly, brown lignite that still contains recognizable plant remains. Undried peat is 90 percent water; lignite is 50 percent.

Coal seams
Layers of coal are called seams. They are sandwiched between layers of other material, such as sandstones and mudstones.

"Black gold"
Under pressure, lignite is converted into bituminous or household coal. Hard and brittle, it has a very high carbon content. A charcoal-like powdery substance makes the coal dirty to handle.

Children in a mine, 1842
During the Industrial Revolution, miners and their children worked long hours underground in terrible conditions.

Mining for coal
Coal has been mined since the Middle Ages. Some mines are open-cast, at the surface, but most are hundreds of feet beneath the land or sea.

The hardest coal
The highest-quality coal is anthracite. Shiny, harder than other coals, and clean to touch, it contains more carbon than the others, and it gives out the most heat and little smoke.

Fossils

Fossils are the evidence of past life preserved in the rocks of the Earth's crust. When an animal or plant is buried in sediment, usually the soft parts rot away, but the hardest parts remain—most fossils consist of the bones or shells of animals, or the leaves or woody parts of plants. In some marine fossils, shells may be replaced by other minerals, or an impression of the insides or outsides may be preserved. Fossils are found in sedimentary rocks, especially limestones and shales.

Muddy rock

Impression of leaf

Beech leaf

Leaf imprint
About 40 million years old, this fossil leaf is similar to the modern beech leaf.

Magnolia le from Mioce perio

Neuropteris—a seed-fern—fossilized in ironstone

Plant fossils
Many fernlike fossils are found in coal-bearing rocks. Formed in the Carboniferous period, they are called Coal Measures fossils. Many are strikingly similar to the ferns that grow today.

Fern from the Carboniferous period

Fronds of a fe called *Asterothe* preserved in sto

Present-day fern

Section of a
Nautilus shell

Nautilus
The nautilus shell is
divided into chambers. By
regulating the gas in these chambers,
the animal moves up or down in the water.

Ancient ancestors
This limestone (right) is about 200 million years old.
It contains the remains of hundreds of ammonites.
These sea creatures had hard, coiled shells, and are now
extinct. Because ammonites changed rapidly and lived in
many areas of the world, they can be used to determine the
relative ages of the rocks in which they occur. The nearest
modern equivalent to the ammonite is the nautilus.

*Ammonite
remains*

A graveyard for snails
This piece of limestone (left) contains
the hard spiral shells of marine
gastropods (snails) from about
120 million years ago.

Impression of interior of shell

Gastropod shell

Fossil hunting
The abundance
of fossils on
seashores made
collecting a
popular pastime
in the 19th
century.

Garden
snails

39

Space rocks

Every year about 19,000 meteorites each weighing over 4 oz (100 g) fall to Earth; most land in the sea or on deserts. Only about five are recovered annually. As they enter Earth's atmosphere, their surfaces melt and are swept away, but their cold interiors survive.

Pasamonte fireball

Photographed in New Mexico, this fireball fell to Earth in March 1933. Meteorites are named after the places where they fall—this one in Pasamonte. The fireball broke up in the atmosphere, heralding the fall of dozens of meteoritic stones.

Metallic meteorite

The Cañon Diablo meteorite landed about 20,000 years ago. Iron meteorites like this one are rarer than stony meteorites and consist of an iron-nickel alloy. They once formed parts of small asteroids that broke up when they collided with Earth. The largest meteorite known is the iron Hoba, from Namibia, which weighs about 66 tons (60 metric tons).

Explosion crater

When the 16,500-ton (15,000-metric ton) Cañon Diablo meteorite hit Arizona, it exploded. It created a huge hole, the Meteor Crater, about ¾ mile (1.2 km) across and nearly 600 ft (180 m) deep. Only 33 tons (30 metric tons) of meteorite remained, scattered as small fragments across the surrounding countryside.

Fragme of meteor

Dark, glas *fusion cru* *formed duri* *passage throu* *Earth's atmosphe*

Gray interior consisting mainly of the minerals olivine and pyroxene

Earth's contempora

The meteorite above fell at Barwe Leicestershire, UK, on Christmas Ev 1965. It formed 4.6 billion years ag at the same time as Earth but another part of the solar system. every 10 meteorites seen to fa eight are "stones" like Barwe

Metal and ston

Stony-irons form a separate gro of meteorites. This slice of the Th Mountains meteorite shows brig metal enclosing stony material was found in Antarctica, whe meteorites have la for about 300,0 years, large encas in ic

Metal

Stony part containing olivine

Halley's Comet

Water-bearing meteorites may have come from comets, such as Halley's—here depicted in the Bayeux tapestry.

Asteroid structure

Many meteorites come from the collision of asteroids that circle the Sun, mostly between the orbits of Mars and Jupiter. They have a metal core, the source of some iron meteorites like Cañon Diablo; a core-mantle, the source of stony-iron meteorites like Thiel Mountains; a mantle, from which few meteorites are known; and an outer crust, the source of stony meteorites like Barwell.

ust

ntle

re-
ntle

re

Water-bearers

The Murchison meteorite fell in Australia in 1969. It contains carbon compounds and water, similar to the nucleus of a comet. Such meteorites are rare.

Rocks from the Moon and Mars

Five meteorites found in Antarctica are known to have come from the Moon because they are like lunar highlands rocks collected by the Apollo missions. Eight other meteorites are thought to have come from Mars.

Martian origin

The Nakhla stone fell in Egypt in 1911. Only 1.3 billion years old, far younger than most meteorites, it probably came from Mars.

Lunar discoveries

The lunar meteorites are made of the same material as this boulder next to Apollo 17 astronaut, Jack Schmitt.

Moon rock

The Moon's surface is covered with soil made of rock and mineral fragments, from bombardment by meteorites. Similar material on the surface of an asteroid was compacted to form stony meteorites. Here, the white minerals are feldspar, the darker ones pyroxene.

Petrological
microscope

Minerals

Eight elements make up nearly 99 percent
of Earth's crust, combining to form minerals
that form rocks. Certain mineral groups are typical of certain rocks.
Silica minerals predominate in common, mostly igneous, rocks.

Crust's makeup
In weight order: oxygen
(1), silicon (2), aluminu
(3), iron (4), calcium (5),
sodium (6), potassium
magnesium (8), and all
other elements (9).

Minerals in granitic rocks

Feldspars, the most common minerals, plus quartz,
micas, and amphiboles form granitic and dioritic rocks.

*Group
of black
prismatic
crystals
with
calcite*

Single
hornblende
crystal

Silica minerals
These include quartz, chalcedony, and opal.
Quartz is one of the most widely distributed
minerals, occuring in igneous, sedimentary,
and metamorphic rocks.

Potassic feldspar
Orthoclase is found
many metamorphic ar
igneous rocks. I
lower-temperatu
form is microclin

Quartz or
rock crystal

Green microcline
(or amazonstone)
crystal

Twinned
crystals of white
orthoclase

Hornblende, an
amphibole, common
in igneous and some
metamorphic rocks

Tremolite, common in
metamorphic
rocks

Thin section of a diorite
Viewed under the special light of a
petrological microscope, this diorite
reveals colored amphiboles, plain gray
to white quartz, and is lined
gray plagioclase feldspar.

Biotite, a dar
iron-rich mica usual
found in igneous roc

*Silvery, radiating,
needlelike crystals*

Amphiboles
This group of minerals is widely
found in igneous and metamorphic
rocks. They can be distinguished
from pyroxenes (opposite) by the
characteristic angles between
their cleavage planes (p.48).

Muscovite,
an aluminum-
rich mica

*Silvery brown
tabular crystals*

Micas
There are two main types of mica: dark
iron- and magnesium-rich mica, and white
aluminum-rich mica. All have perfect
cleavage, splitting into thin flakes.

Basic rocks

The minerals shown here are all found in basic rocks like basalts and gabbros.

Pink crystals of anorthite, a plagioclase feldspar, with augite

Twinned crystals of albite with calcite

Olivine
This silicate of iron and magnesium is typically found in silica-poor rocks, such as basalts, gabbros, and peridotites. It often forms as small grains or large, granular masses.

Green olivine crystals

Crystals of olivine, from Vesuvius

Single crystal of augite

Nepheline, a feldspathoid, with calcite

Thin section of a basalt
Olivine basalt reveals brightly colored olivine, brown-yellow pyroxene, and minute gray plagioclase feldspars.

Plagioclase feldspars
Common in igneous rocks, these minerals (above) contain sodium and calcium.

Feldspathoids
These minerals have less silica than feldspars and typically form in volcanic lavas.

Volcanic rock

Crystal of leucite, a feldspathoid

Prismatic crystal of enstatite with biotite

Greenish-black prismatic crystals of augite, a pyroxene

Pyroxenes
The most common pyroxenes are calcium, magnesium, and iron silicates. Augite is a widely distributed pyroxene. Enstatite is less common.

Other groups

Carbonates and clays are two more groups of rock-forming minerals.

Carbonates
These are key constituents of sedimentary (limestones) or metamorphic (marble) rocks. The most common is calcite, in limestones.

Dolomite, a carbonate, found in some sedimentary deposits usually interbedded with limestones

Montmorillonite

Illite

Kaolinite (china clay) formed from partly decomposed orthoclase

Clays
Part of the sedimentary rock sequence, clays form from the weathering and alteration of aluminous silicates.

Crystals

Snowflake

The word crystal comes from the Greek word *kryos*, meaning icy cold—rock crystal, a form of quartz, was once thought to be deep-frozen ice. In fact, a crystal is a solid, with a regular internal structure. Due to the arrangement of its atoms, it may form smooth external surfaces called faces. Many crystals have commercial uses, and some are cut as gemstones.

Crystal collecting in the Alps, c. 1870

Crystals orientated in random growth directions

Light reflecting on the crystal face

Parallel striations (lines) formed as the crystal grew

Large twinned crystal

Plane of intersection

Well developed faces

"Ice" sculpted by nature

This beautiful group of rock crystal found in Isère, France, is particular well formed, consisting of a large twin crystal and many simple crystals. The narrow ridges and furrows across some of its faces ar called striations. These were forme when two different crystal faces trie to develop at the same time.

Crystal symmetry

rystals can be grouped into seven systems according
their symmetry, which is shown in certain regular
atures of the crystal. For example, for every face
ere may be another on the opposite side of the
ystal that is parallel to it and similar in shape and
ze. But in most mineral specimens it can be difficult
determine the symmetry because crystals occur
aggregates and do not have well developed faces.

What's the angle?
Since the angle between
corresponding faces
of a particular mineral
is always the same,
scientists measure the
angle with a contact
goniometer to help
identify the mineral.

Reading of angle

The angle between crystal faces being measured

riclinic
is system's crystals display the least symmetry,
shown by this wedge-shaped axinite crystal.

Cubic
Metallic pyrite forms cube-shaped
crystals, but other cubic mineral
forms include octahedra and
tetrahedra. Crystals in this system
exhibit the highest symmetry.

Tetragonal
Dark-green vesuvianite
crystals are grouped with
zircon and wulfenite in
the tetragonal system.

Rhombohedral (trigonal)
Smaller secondary crystals have grown on this
siderite crystal. Quartz, tourmaline, corundum,
and calcite belong to the same system.

Orthorhombic
Common crystals in
this sytem include
olivine, topaz, and
baryte (right), the
source of barium
for medical use.

onoclinic
e most common crystal system
cludes gypsum (from which
e make plaster of Paris),
urite, and orthoclase.

Hexagonal
Beryl, including this emerald
variety, crystallizes in the
hexagonal system, as do apatite
and ice and snowflakes.

Snowflakes

winning

cavities in mineral veins,
ystals may grow in
oups. Sometimes
o (or possibly
ore) individual
ystals appear
intersect in a
mmetrical manner;
ese are known as
winned crystals."

Contact twins
The mineral cerussite crystallizes
in the orthorhombic system, like
this group of twin crystals (left).

Penetration twins
Staurolite is also an orthorhombic
mineral. In this cross-shaped
specimen, one twin appears
to penetrate into the other.

**Twinned gypsum crystals form
an arrow-shape from which
they get their common name,
"swallow-tail"**

Crystal growth

No two crystals are exactly alike because the conditions in which they develop vary. They range from microscopic to several yards long. The shape of a crystal or aggregate of crystals constitute its "habit."

Coral-like shape

White coral
Aragonite, named after the Spanish province of Aragon, can sometimes hav a "coralloid" (coral-shaped) habit.

Fine crystal "needles"

Radiating needles
Slender, elongated crystals are said to have an "acicular" (needlelike) habit. In this scolecite specimen, gray acicular crystals radiate from the center.

Metallic "grapes"
Some chalcopyrite crystals grow outward from a center and such aggregates appear as rounded nodules. The habit is "botryoidal meaning "like a bunch of grapes

Sparkling aggregate
Hematite occurs in several habits. When it forms shiny, reflective crystals, it is said to have a "specular" habit, as in this aggregate.

Long, rectangular prism faces

Short, hexagonal terminal face at each end

Crystal columns
"Prismatic" crystals, such as this beryl crystal, are muc longer in one direction than in the other two.

Equant garnet crysta

Mica schis

Soft strands
These crystals of tremolite are very soft and pliable. Minerals with this habit are known as asbestos.

Thin sheets
Mica splits into sheets and is said to be "micaceous" or "foliated" (leaflike) or "lamellar" (thin and plated).

Equal side
Many minerals develop crystals th are essentially equal in all dimension these are said to be "equan This specimen of garnet in mi schist is a fine examp

...ual form

...rite crystallizes as cubes and as 12-faced ...lids called pentagonal dodecahedra. If the ...nditions change during growth, both forms ...ay codevelop, with striations on the faces.

Strongly striated, cubic faces

Sloping dodecahedral faces

Top of glistening pink calcite crystal group

Base of gray calcite crystal group

Parallel lines

During crystal growth a series of crystals of the same type may develop in the same direction. This calcite aggregate shows a number of tapering pale pink and gray crystals in perfect parallel orientation.

Stepped crystals

This halite contains numerous sand grains. It grew along preferred axes, forming a stack of cubic crystals in steps.

Double-decker

Chalcopyrite and ...halerite crystals have similar structures. ...ere, tarnished, brassy chalcopyrite crystals ...ave grown in parallel on brownish-black sphalerite crystals.

Sphalerite crystals

Chalcopyrite crystals

Sandy cubes

...ranching metal

...a restricted space, as between two beds of ...ck, native copper and other minerals may ...ow in thin sheets. Its characteristic ...anchlike form is described ..."dendritic."

...anches" f copper

Salt lake, Cyprus

When salt lakes dry up, a thick crust of soluble salts is left.

Stepped faces

Hopper growth

The mineral halite (salt) is cubic, but crystals can grow from solution faster along the cube edge than in the center of the faces, resulting in the formation of "hopper crystals" that have stepped cavities in each face.

Outline of chlorite

Phantom growth

The dark areas within this quartz crystal formed when a thin layer of chlorite coated the crystal at an earlier stage of its growth. As the crystal continued to grow, the chlorite became a ghostlike outline.

The properties of minerals

Most minerals have a regular crystal structure and a definite chemical composition. These determine the chemical and physical properties that are characteristic for each mineral and help geologists to identify it and see how it was formed.

Structure

Some chemically identical minerals exist in more than one form. For example, the element carbon forms two minerals: diamond and graphite.

Carbon atom

Model of graphite structure

Model of diamond structure

Carbon atom

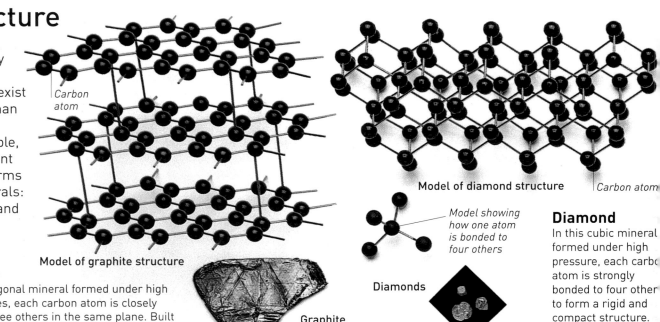

Model showing how one atom is bonded to four others

Diamonds

Graphite
In this hexagonal mineral formed under high temperatures, each carbon atom is closely linked to three others in the same plane. Built up of widely spaced layers only weakly bonded together, graphite is very soft (Mohs' scale 1–2).

Graphite specimen

Diamond
In this cubic mineral formed under high pressure, each carbon atom is strongly bonded to four others to form a rigid and compact structure. Diamond is extremely hard (Mohs' scale 10).

Cleavage

When crystals break, some tend to split along well-defined cleavage planes, due to their atoms' orderly arrangement.

Thin layers

Thin sheets
Stibnite shows a sheetlike cleavage due to weakly bonded chains of antimony and sulfur atoms.

Lead steps
Galena, the main ore of lead, has a cubic cleavage, due to the arrangement of its lead and sulfur atoms. A split face has small cubic steps.

Steps

Perfect break
Baryte crystals show two perfect cleavages. If this crystal were broken, it would split along these planes.

Thin lines show cleavage planes

Smaller crystal growing with larger crystal

Perfect rhomb
Calcite has such a well developed rhombohedral cleavage that a break in any other direction is virtually impossible.

Fracture
Quartz crystals break with a glassy, conchoidal (shell-like) fracture, not along a particular plane.

Rounded, conchoidal edges

Hardness

The bonds holding atoms together dictate a mineral's hardness. In 1812, mineralogist Friedrich Mohs devised a scale of hardness that is still in use today. He chose 10 minerals as standards and ranked them so that any mineral on the scale would scratch only those below it.

Relative hardness
The intervals between the minerals in Mohs' scale are irregular. Diamond is about 40 times harder than talc, while corundum is only nine times as hard.

1	2	3	4	5	6	7	8	9	10
Talc	Gypsum	Calcite	Fluorite	Apatite	Orthoclase	Quartz	Topaz	Corundum	Diamond

Magnetism

Only two common minerals, magnetite and pyrrhotite (both iron compounds), are strongly magnetic. Magnetite lodestones were used as an early form of compass.

Natural magnet
Permanently magnetized magnetite attracts iron filings and other metallic objects such as paper clips.

Clusters of iron filings

Optical

The optical effect as light passes through a mineral is due to light's interaction with atoms in the structure.

Double daisy
Light traveling through a calcite rhomb is split into two rays, which makes one stem look like two.

Fluorescing autunite
Viewed under ultraviolet light, certain minerals fluoresce.

Specific gravity

Specific gravity is defined as the ratio of the weight of a substance to that of an equal volume of water. Determining the specific gravity may aid identification.

Size vs. weight
The nature of the atoms and internal atomic arrangement of a mineral determines its specific gravity. These three mineral specimens are different sizes but weigh the same, as the atoms in quartz and galena are heavier or more closely packed together than the atoms in mica.

Mica

Quartz

Galena

Gemstones

Gemstones are minerals of great beauty, rarity, and resilience. Light reflects and refracts with the minerals to produce the intense colors of gems, such as ruby and emerald, and the "fire" of diamond. Color, fire, and luster are revealed by skilled cutting and polishing for use in jewelry. Gems are usually weighed by the carat, equal to one-fifth of a gram.

Gem-studded ornament

Beryl

Beautiful, hexagonal beryl crystals are found in many countries. Emerald and aquamarine, two major gem varieties, have long been exploited. Egyptian emerald mines date back to 1650 BCE.

Cut emerald

Emeralds
The best emeralds, like those in the British Crown Jewels, occur in veins with calcite and pyrite, in Colombia. Flawless emeralds are very rare and most crystals contain small blemishes or mineral inclusions.

Roman beryl
The earrings and necklaces contain cut emeralds.

Beryl's assorted colors
Pure beryl is colorless. The gems' colors are due to impurities, such as the manganese that makes morganite pink. Aquamarine can be made bluer with heat.

Yellow heliodor

Greenish heliodor

Aquamarine

Pink morganite

Diamond

Diamond is named from the Greek word *adamas* ("unconquerable"). It is the hardest mineral of all and is famed for its lasting fiery brilliance. The quality of a gem diamond is measured by the four Cs: its color, clarity, cut, and carat weight.

Kimberley diamond mine, South Africa

Treasures in gravel
Until 1870 diamond crystals and fragments came from river gravels, mostly in India or Brazil. The South Africa's diamond-rich kimberlite made it the leading supplier.

Diamond crystal

Kimberlite

Diamonds in rock
Kimberlite is the source rock for most diamonds. It is named after Kimberley in South Africa, where it occurs in a volcanic pipe that has its roots 100–200 miles (160–320 km) deep in Earth's crust.

Multi-colored diamonds
Diamonds range from colorless through yellow and brown to pink, green, blue, and a very rare red. Table, rose, and brilliant cuts display their fire and luster to best advantage.

Crown jewel
The Koh-i-noor Indian diamond, worn here by Queen Mary, was given to Queen Victoria in 1850.

Corundum

Ruby and sapphire are varieties of the mineral corundum, which is colorless when pure. Tiny quantities of chromium give rise to the red of ruby. Iron and titanium give the blues, yellows, and greens of sapphire.

Star sapphire

Stones with fine, needlelike crystals orientated in three directions can be cut as star rubies or star sapphires.

The Edwardes Ruby

This exceptional crystal weighs 162 carats. It is almost certainly from the famous gem deposits of Mogok, Myanmar (Burma).

Cut ruby

Gem sources

Australia supplies the most blue and yellow sapphires. Rubies are mined in Myanmar, Thailand, and central Africa. Sri Lanka is famous for blue and pink sapphires.

Sapphire crystal

Ruby tends to form in flat crystals, while sapphire tends to be barrel-shaped or pyramidal, often with zones of blue to yellow color.

River jewels

Most sapphires and rubies come from gem-rich gravels. The gems are harder and less weathered than the parent rocks filtered out in riverbeds.

Gems in jewelry

The oldest jewelry comes from burials 20,000 years ago. Here, rubies, emeralds, and diamonds decorate a late-16th-century enameled, gold pendant.

Blue sapphire

Colorless sapphire

Pink sapphire

Yellow sapphire

Clear sapphire

Mauve sapphire

Opal

Opal probably gets its name from India, from the Sanskrit word *upala* ("precious stone"). Roman jewelry used opals from the Czech Republic. In the 1500s, opal came from Central America. After 1870, Australia became the leading supplier.

Opal mining in Australia

In addition to its use in jewelry, opal mined today is also used in the manufacture of abrasives and insulation products.

Color variations in opal

Opal's blue, green, yellow, and red iridescence is caused by light from minute silica spheres within the mineral. The "body" color can be clear, milky, white, or either gray or black in its most precious form.

Iridescent black opals

White opal

Milky opal

Fire opal

The finest fire opal comes from Mexico and Turkey and is usually cut as faceted stones. It is valued as much for its intensity of color as for its iridescence.

Opal's rocky origins

Most opal forms over long periods of time in sedimentary rocks, like this sample from Australia, but in Mexico and the Czech Republic it forms in gas cavities in volcanic rocks. Opal is often cut as cabochons, but the veins in sedimentary rocks are often thin. Slices may be glued onto onyx or glass to form doublets, and capped with clear quartz to form a triplet.

Decorative stones

Turquoise, agate, lapis lazuli, and jade are all gems made up of many crystals. They are valued mainly for their color, evenly distributed as in turquoise, or patterned as in an agate cameo. Agate and jade are also tough, ideal for fine carving.

Chalcedony

Cornelian, onyx, chrysoprase, and agate are all forms of chalcedony. Pure chalcedony is translucent gray or white and consists of thin layers of tiny quartz fibers. Impurities create the patterns in agate.

Chrysopra caboch

Ancient favorite
Apple-green chrysoprase has bee used in jewelry since pre-Roman times, often in cameos or intaglio

Vein of turquoise

Lapis lazuli

This blue gem consists mainly of lazurite and sodalite minerals with white calcite and specks of brassy-colored pyrite.

Purest samples
The best lapis lazuli is mined in Badakhshan, Afghanistan, where it occurs in lenses and veins in white marble.

Turquoise

Found in the earliest jewelry, turquoise gives its name to "turquoise-blue," a pale greenish-blue. Its color is largely due to copper and traces of iron. The more iron present, the greener the stone.

Lapis jewelry
Long used for beads and carvings, lapis has been known for more than 6,000 years and is named from the Persian word *Lazhward* ("blue").

Mesopotamian mosaic
Lapis was used to decorate the wooden box known as the Standard of Ur (detail above), c. 2,500 BCE.

Egyptian amul
Many fine carvings ha been recover from the tom of Egypt pharao

Cut turquoise
The finest sky-blue turquoise has been mined in Nishapur, Iran, for 3,000 years. Another ancient source, known to the Aztecs, is in the US Southwest, which now supplies most of the world's turquoise.

Turquoise ornaments
This artifact may be of Persian origin. The double-headed serpent (top) is from an Aztec necklace.

True blue
The vivid blue of this lapis slice (left) is caused by small amounts of sulfur.

Agate
Banded agates form in cavities in volcanic rocks. Uruguay and Brazil are prolific sources.

Crystals

Polished sliced agate
Microscopic crystals formed in bands as hot, silica-rich solutions filtered through cavities in porous rocks.

Cameo portrait
This bloodstone shows a Roman emperor.

Deep-colored band

Ornamental knife
Cornelian is red chalcedony and has been used in jewelry and inlay work throughout history.

Stone landscape
The pattern in moss agate or mocha stone is shown to advantage in this delicate cabochon.

Jade
Named from the Spanish *piedra de hijada* used to describe the green stone carved by the Indians in Central America, jade refers to two different substances—jadeite and nephrite.

Mogul dagger
Mogul craftsmen carved pale green and gray nephrite into dagger handles, bowls, and jewelry, often inlaid with rubies and other gems.

...utankhamun's mask
...pis, cornelian, obsidian, ...artz, and colored glass are ...aid in gold.

Rare jade
Jadeite can be white, orange, brown, lilac, or the translucent green "imperial jade."

Chinese art
The toughness of jade was known to the Chinese more than 2,000 years ago and this was exploited in their delicate carvings.

Nephrite boulder
Nephrite is more common than jadeite and is generally green, gray, or creamy white. Much jade occurs as waterworn boulders, as in this example from New Zealand.

Other gems

In addition to well-known gemstones such as diamond, ruby, sapphire, emerald, and opal, many other minerals have been used for human adornment. These are just some of the stones frequently seen in jewelry, but the full range of luster, fire, and color is extensive.

Mughal emperor Shah Jahan

Multicolored topaz

Blue topaz

Yell￼
top

Topaz

Occuring chiefly in granites and pegmatites, some gem-quality topaz crystals are very large, weighing many pounds. The largest stones are colorless or pale blue, but the most valuable are golden-yellow imperial topaz or pink topaz.

Blue spinel

Pink spinel

Mauve spinel

Spinel

Red spinels resemble rubies and were once called balas rubies, after Balascia, now Badakhshan in Afghanistan. There is also a range of pink, lilac, blue, and bluish-green stones.

Cut spinel

Black Prince's Ruby

This famous spinel is the central stone in the British Imperial State Crown.

Topaz brooch

Brown topaz was commonly used in 18th- and 19th-century jewelry. Yellow topaz was heated to turn it pink.

Perid￼

This is the transparent gem variety olivine. The proportion of iron in the miner￼ determines the shade of color. The mo￼ valuable golden-green and deep-gre￼ stones contain less iron than those w￼ a brownish tinge. Peridot ha￼ been used in jewelry sin￼ classical times, ar￼ originally came from t￼ island of Zebirget ￼ the Red Se￼

Vermilion zircon

Pink zircon

Green zircon

Yellow zircon

Blue zircon

Zircon

Named from *zargoon*, the Arabic word for vermilion or golden colored, stones of these colors as well as green and brown have long been used in Indian jewelry. Transparent stones are cut and polished for a luster and fire similar to diamond, but they are softer and chip more easily.

Cut peridots

Garnet

Garnet is a group name for a diverse set of gems that includes [al]mandine and pyrope (red and purplish-red), spessartine [o]range-red), grossular (orange, green, or colorless), and [d]emantoid (green). Fine demantoid rivals emerald for color and exceeds diamond for fire. Its beauty and rarity command a high price.

Grossular garnets

Garnet earrings
Rose-cut stones make attractive jewelry when set in gold, as shown by these 18th-century earrings.

Rose-cut stone

Gold

Almandine   Hessonite   Pyrope   Demantoid

Demantoid garnets

Greek diadem
[Th]is section of an Hellenistic diadem dates from the [secon]d century BCE and is inlaid with garnets. Its design [is] common to many Greek artifacts of that time.

Tourmaline
[To]urmaline shows the greatest range in color of any gemstone, and [so]me single crystals are multicolored. The crystal forms and [ele]ctrical properties are different at each end of a crystal—this [dis]parity is sometimes reflected in color differences, especially pink [an]d green. Cut stones can show this variation to advantage.

19th-century amethyst necklace

Amethyst
Purple amethyst is a variety of quartz. Colorless, transparent rock crystal is the purest form of quartz, and the colors of amethyst, citrine (yellow quartz), and rose quartz are caused by iron or titanium impurities.

Cut amethyst

[Yel]lowish-[gr]een [tou]rmaline   Green tourmaline   Blue tourmaline   Pink tourmaline   Brown tourmaline   Mauve-gray tourmaline   "Watermelon" tourmaline

Graduating color tourmaline

Byzantine relic, c. 955 CE
Many Byzantine artifacts were made of gold and decorated with precious stones.

Ore minerals

Mined, quarried, or dredged from lakes and rivers, ore minerals are crushed and separated, then refined and smelted (fused and melted) to produce metal. Copper was in use well before 5000 BCE. Around 3000 BCE, tin was added to make a harder metal, bronze. Iron was even harder and was widespread by 500 BCE.

Bronze ritual food vessel from China, c. 10th century BCE

Bauxite— aluminum ore

Iron mining, c. 15•

Lightweight aluminum
Aluminum is a good conductor of electricity, lightweight, not easily corroded, and used in power lines and saucepans.

Aluminum foil

Stacks of aluminum ingots

Hematite— iron ore

Tough iro
Hematite is the most importa iron ore. Iron is tough and ha yet easy to work. It can be ca forged, machined, rolled, a alloyed with other meta Steel is made from iro

Steel screw

Rutile—titanium ore

Strong titanium
Rutile and ilmenite are the main ores of titanium. Usually found in igneous or metamorphic rocks, these two minerals form deposits with other minerals, many of which are extracted as by-products. Lightweight yet very strong, titanium is widely used in aircraft frames and engines.

Colorful copper
Brassy, yellow chalcopyrite and bluish-purple bornite are common copper ores. Because it is a good conductor, copper is used in the electricity industry, and because it is malleable (easy to shape and roll), it is good for household water pipes. It is also used in alloys with zinc (brass) and with tin (bronze).

Chalcopyrit

Born coppe ore

Copper plumbing joint

Airliner partially constructed from titanium

**Galvanized
nail**

Sphalerite—
zinc ore

Durable nickel

Nickel comes from deposits in large, layered gabbroic intrusions and from deposits formed by the weathering of basaltic igneous rocks. Nickeline occurs in small amounts in silver and uranium deposits where nickel is a by-product. Nickel is used in corrosion-resistant alloys, such as stainless steel and in high-temperature, high-strength alloys suitable for aircraft and jet engines.

Nickeline—
nickel ore

Nickel alloy
battery

Cinnabar—
mercury ore

Black jack zinc

Sphalerite or "black jack," as it was known by miners, is the most important zinc ore and is found in deposits in volcanic and sedimentary rocks. Zinc is used in galvanizing—coating sheet steel with a thin layer of zinc to prevent it from rusting.

Zinc processing in
Belgium, c. 1873

Red mercury

The poisonous mercury ore cinnabar forms close to recent volcanic rocks and hot springs. Mercury is very dense, has a low melting point, and is liquid at room temperature. It is widely used in drugs, pigments, insecticides, and scientific instruments.

Mercury
thermometer

Soft and shiny lead

Galena, the main lead ore, is worked chiefly from deposits in limestones. Lead is the densest and softest common metal, with high resistance to corrosion, but it is not very strong. Is used in storage batteries, gas, engineering and plumbing, and with tin in solder.

Lead solder

Galena—
lead ore

19th-century tin mine in
Cornwall, UK

Crystalline
cassiterite—
tin ore

Tin can, more
often made
of aluminum

Workable tin

The tin ore cassiterite is hard, heavy, and resistant to abrasion. Modern uses of tin are based on its resistance to corrosion, low melting point, malleability, lack of toxicity, and high conductivity. It is used in solder and tinplate. Pewter is an alloy with roughly 75 percent tin and 25 percent lead.

Precious metals

Gold and silver were among the first metals discovered. Valued for beauty and rarity, they—and platinum in the last 100 years—are used in coins to prove wealth, buy, and sell, and in jewelry and other objects.

Platinum

Now more valuable than gold, platinum is used in oil refining and in reducing pollution from car exhausts.

Sperrylite crystal
Platinum is found in several minerals, one being sperrylite. This is the largest known sperrylite crystal, found in South Africa c. 1924.

Platinum grains
Most platinum minerals occur as tiny grains in nickel deposits. These grains are from Colombia, where platinum was first reported in the 18th century.

Imperial coins
Platinum has been used as coinage in several countries, including Russia.

Platinum nugget
Large nuggets of platinum are rare. This one, from Nizhni-Tagil in the Urals, weighs 2 lb 6½ oz (1.1 kg), but the largest on record is 21 lb (9.7 kg).

Silver

Long used in coinage, but less valuable than gold or platinum, silver tarnishes easily. Sterling and plated silver are made into jewelry and ornaments.

Mexican ore-crusher
Early methods of crushing silver ore were primitive but effective.

Delicate silver wires
Silver is now mostly extracted as a by-product from copper and lead-zinc mining. Until the 20th century, it was mostly mined as native metal, like the famous silver "wires" from Norway.

Celtic brooch
The Celts fashioned many intricate pieces of jewelry in silver.

Silver branches
Occasionally, as in this specimen from Copiapo, Chile, silver occurs in delicate branchlike dendritic forms.

Religious bell
One of a pair, this silver Torah bell was made in Italy in the early 18th century and was used in Jewish ceremonies.

Gold

Today, this metal is used in jewelry, electronics, and dentistry, but more than half the gold mined is buried again—in bank vaults, as investments.

Crystalline chalcopyrite

South Africa
Traditional gold mines were labor intensive.

The Great Gold Rush
Prospectors flocked to pan gold in 19th-century California, the Yukon, Canada, and Australia.

Fool's gold
Pyrite and chalcopyrite's brassy color can be mistaken for gold. But chalcopyrite, the main ore of copper, is more greenish-yellow, more brittle, and harder than gold, although not as hard as pyrite.

Massive chalcopyrite

Vein gold
Gold may occur in quartz veins. It is extracted by crushing the ore for a concentrate, which is then smelted.

Pyrite
Pyrite mostly forms cubic crystals and is closer in color to "white gold" or electrum, an alloy of gold and silver, than to pure gold.

Tutankhamun's collar

Gold grains
Gold is also produced by smelting particles that have been dredged or panned then separated out from gravel and sand deposits.

Crystalline pyrite

Egyptian craft
The ancient Egyptians were one of the first civilizations to master the art of goldsmithing, using solid, beaten gold. Today, copper and silver are often added to gold (measured in carats) to make it harder.

Massive pyrite

Cutting and polishing

The earliest gemstones were rubbed together to produce a smooth surface, which could then be engraved. Much later, professional craftsmen (lapidaries) became skilled at cutting precious stones to maximize their optical effect and size.

Grinding and polishing agates in a German workshop c. 1800

Cutting gems

When mined, gemstones often look dull. To create a desirable, sparkling gem, the lapidary must cut and polish it to enhance its natural qualities, allowing for any flaws within.

The hardest cut
Rough diamonds are marked with indian ink before cutting.

Popular cuts
The first, simple cuts included table and cabochon cuts. More complex, faceted cuts include the brilliant for diamond and other colorless stones.

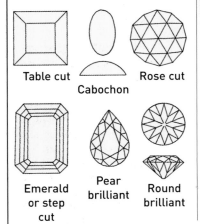

Table cut

Cabochon

Rose cut

Emerald or step cut

Pear brilliant

Round brilliant

Hollow drum rotated by rollers

Belt driven by motor

Lid of drum

Rollers

Tumbling
Amateur lapidaries use a tumbling machine to rub pieces of mineral with coarse grit and water for about a week, then with finer grits until the pebbles are rounded and polished.

Tumbling action
As the drum rotates, pebbles are rubbed smooth and round.

Rough mineral pieces ready for tumbling

Grits and polishes
Grinding grits are used in sequence, from the coarsest to the finest.

Water added with grits

Coarse grinding grit used in first tumbling

Fine grinding grit for second tumbling

Cerium oxide, fine polishing powder finally makes pebbles smooth and sparkling

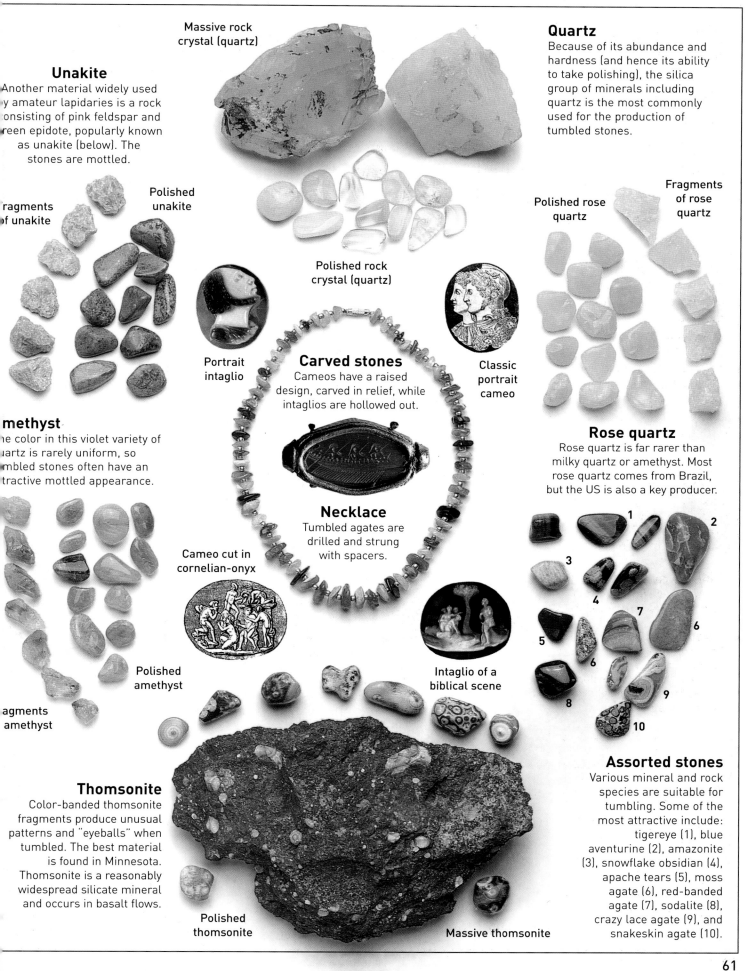

Unakite

Another material widely used by amateur lapidaries is a rock consisting of pink feldspar and green epidote, popularly known as unakite (below). The stones are mottled.

Fragments of unakite

Polished unakite

Massive rock crystal (quartz)

Polished rock crystal (quartz)

Quartz

Because of its abundance and hardness (and hence its ability to take polishing), the silica group of minerals including quartz is the most commonly used for the production of tumbled stones.

Polished rose quartz

Fragments of rose quartz

Portrait intaglio

Carved stones

Cameos have a raised design, carved in relief, while intaglios are hollowed out.

Classic portrait cameo

Amethyst

The color in this violet variety of quartz is rarely uniform, so tumbled stones often have an attractive mottled appearance.

Necklace

Tumbled agates are drilled and strung with spacers.

Rose quartz

Rose quartz is far rarer than milky quartz or amethyst. Most rose quartz comes from Brazil, but the US is also a key producer.

Cameo cut in cornelian-onyx

Polished amethyst

Fragments of amethyst

Intaglio of a biblical scene

Thomsonite

Color-banded thomsonite fragments produce unusual patterns and "eyeballs" when tumbled. The best material is found in Minnesota. Thomsonite is a reasonably widespread silicate mineral and occurs in basalt flows.

Polished thomsonite

Massive thomsonite

Assorted stones

Various mineral and rock species are suitable for tumbling. Some of the most attractive include: tigereye (1), blue aventurine (2), amazonite (3), snowflake obsidian (4), apache tears (5), moss agate (6), red-banded agate (7), sodalite (8), crazy lace agate (9), and snakeskin agate (10).

Starting a collection

Collecting mineral and rock specimens is a rewarding and popular pastime. It dates back to the amateur geologists of the 19th century, many of whom amassed impressive collections.

Satchel with rock specimens

Collecting tools
You need a geological hammer, weighing 1–2 lb (0.5–1 kg), and a range of chisels. Geological hammers usually have a square head on one and a chisel on the other side. Do not use ordinary hammers, which may splinter.

Club hammer for use with chisels

Geologist's hammer (1 lb/0.5 kg)

Wide-ended chisel

Sharp, pointed chisel

Geologist's trimming hammer

Careful planning
Plan any field work and collecting trips in advance, using geological guidebooks and maps. Get permission to visit any area or site on private land. If alone, make sure someone knows your intended route and destination. Always carry a compass and give a grid reference in your field notes.

Map

Compass

Guide book

Field work
Geologists in the 19th century developed the techniques of collecting and mapping rocks.

Protective clothing
To prevent injury from flying rock and metal splinters, wear the protective gear shown here, stout shoes or boots, and strong, waterproof clothing.

Strong gloves

Safety helmet

Protective goggles

Warning

When rock-collecting, there are certain rules you should follow at all times: always obey local laws, ask permission before entering private land, do not disturb wildlife, wear suitable clothing, use proper equipment, and make sure not to create hazards for others.

Recording a find

Number the specimen with a pen or tape and record the exact locality and details in a notebook, with a photo or sketch.

Notebook

Pencil

Pen

Identification

In the field, use a 10 magnification hand lens. Indoors, a binocular microscope will reveal finer details.

Camera to record site or location of find—when taking photographs, try to include something to show scale

Spatulas for fine work, such as cutting around fossils

Surgical knife for fine preparatory work on fossils

Palette knife for extracting small crystals from soft fossils

Sample bag   **Newspaper**

Plastic tube

Transporting

Wrap each specimen individually to prevent chipping or scratching. Since crystal groups are usually very fragile, pack them in tubes or boxes with wrapping and carry in collecting bags.

Bubble wrap

Sealable plastic bag

Fine work

To remove surplus rock from a specimen, wash in water and scrub lightly with a soft brush. Or sift crumbly rock like clay for small crystals and bits of rock.

Curating your collection

To prevent damage to specimens, store in individual trays or boxes in shallow drawers. Bear in mind their individual needs—some minerals deteriorate in damp, heat, or light.

Trowel for digging soft rocks

Sieve for sorting material

Paintbrushes for cleaning specimens

Boxes for storing specimens   Labels for documenting specimens

Did you know?

AMAZING FACTS

After astronauts returned from the Moon, scientists discovered that the most common type of lunar rock is a basalt also found on Earth.

Spider fossilized in amber

Amber formed when sticky resin oozed from trees millions of years ago, sometimes trapping insects before it hardened.

The deeper into the crust a tunnel goes, the hotter it becomes. The deepest gold mines in South Africa have to be cooled down artificially so that people are able to work in them.

Devil's Tower, Wyoming

Devil's Tower, in Wyoming is a huge rock pillar made from lava that crystallized inside the vent of a volcano. Over thousands of years, the softer rock of the volcano itself has worn away.

More than 75 percent of the Earth's crust is made of silicates, minerals that are composed of silicon, oxygen, and some metals.

On some coastlines made up of soft rocks, the sea carves away yards of land every year. Some villages, such as Dunwich in Suffolk, UK, have partly fallen into the sea as cliffs collapsed.

Ice can shatter rock. Granite, one of the hardest rocks, can be split by water in cracks expanding as it freezes. The combined weight and movement of a glacier (a river of ice) can hollow out a whole mountainside.

Unaware it was poisonous, women in ancient Rome used the mineral arsenic as a cosmetic to whiten their skin.

Graphite, used in pencils, is also used in nuclear power plants. Huge graphite rods help to control the speed of nuclear reactions in the reactor core.

Obsidian is a black, volcanic rock that is so shiny that it was used as a mirror in ancient times.

Rocks are constantly changed by erosion and forces deep inside the Earth. Water and wind have carved out this sandstone arch over millions of years.

Obsidian

Rock arch in Utah

Fossil of *Archaeopteryx*

In 1861, a quarryman discovered the fossil of a birdlike creature with feathers that lived 150 million years ago. *Archaeopteryx* may link prehistoric reptiles and today's birds.

Minerals don't just exist in rocks. Your bones are made of minerals, too!

Q What are the most common rocks in the Earth's crust?

A Volcanic rocks, such as basalt, are the most common crustal rocks. Basalt forms from the more fluid type of lava as it cools and hardens. It makes up the ocean floors, which cover 68 percent of Earth's surface.

Q How do we know that dinosaurs existed?

A Dinosaur bones and teeth have been found as fossils in rocks all over the world (as have other animals and plants). Even their footprints and dung have been preserved in rock.

Chinese nephrite dragon

Q What is jade, and why has it got more than one name?

A In 1863, this rock was found to be two different minerals, now called jadeite and nephrite.

Q Why are the pebbles on a beach so many different colors?

A Pebbles are made up of many types of rock, washed up from many places. Their colors show what kinds of minerals they contain.

Fossilized footprint of a dinosaur

Q If pumice is a rock, why does it can float on water?

A Pumice is hardened lava froth from volcanoes on land and under the sea. It is full of tiny air bubbles—the air trapped inside these bubbles makes pumice light enough to float on water.

Q What made the stripes on the desert rocks in Utah?

A The rocks are made of layers of sandstone. Over millions of years, hot days, cold nights, floods, and storms have worn away the softer layers of rock, creating stripes in the landscape.

Badlands, Utah

Q What are the oldest rocks on the planet?

A The oldest known rocks came from space as meteorites. This chondrite is 4.6 billion years old. The first rocks to form on Earth are only 4.2 billion years old.

Chondrite

Q Are there new any rocks forming on Earth?

A New rocks form all the time: some from layers of sediment, others from volcanic activity under water and on land. Rock is constantly recycled by heat, pressure, and erosion.

Q What is a desert rose made from and how did it form?

A Desert rose is made of gypsum. It formed when water quickly evaporated, leaving impurities that formed crystals shaped like petals.

Desert rose

Record Breakers

MOST VALUABLE METAL
Platinum is the most valuable metal, more valuable than gold.

BIGGEST GOLD NUGGET
The largest gold nugget on record weighed 156 lb 6 oz (70.9 kg)—as heavy as a man.

MOST VALUABLE RELIGIOUS ITEM
The Golden Buddha of Bangkok is made of 6.1 tons (5.5 metric tons) of solid gold.

HARDEST MINERAL
Diamond is the hardest known mineral and cannot be scratched by any other.

BIGGEST STALAGMITE
A stalagmite in Krasnohorska, Slovakia, is 103 ft (31.5 m) tall.

BIGGEST ROCK
Uluru (Ayer's Rock) in Australia is the biggest freestanding rock in the world. It is 2¼ miles (3.6 km) long.

Rock or mineral?

Geologists classify rocks according to the way in which they were formed, in three main types: igneous, metamorphic, and sedimentary rocks.

Geologist's tools

IDENTIFYING ROCKS

Igneous rocks

Igneous rocks are made from hot, molten rock from deep within the Earth that has solidified as it has cooled. The more slowly a rock has cooled and solidified, the larger the crystals that have formed within it.

Large crystals of quartz, feldspar, and mica formed as the rock slowly cooled

Granite

Large crystals sthat formed as the rock cooled

Gabbro

Dark, fine-grained volcanic rock that formed from lava

Basalt

Glassy volcanic rock that cooled too quickly to form crystals

Obsidian

Metamorphic rocks

New metamorphic rocks form when sedimentary, igneous, or existing metamorphic rocks are transformed by heat and pressure in Earth's crust. The degree of heat is reflected by the size of crystals the minerals form.

Crinkled layers

Folded schist

Fine grain size

Slate

Dark and light bands of color

Gneiss

Sedimentary rocks

Sedimentary rocks are usually made from particles weathered and eroded from other rocks. The particles, from sand grains to boulders, are deposited in layers (strata) and slowly become rocks. These rocks can contain fossils.

Large, coarse pebbles cemented together

Conglomerate

Iron oxide produces orange color

Sandstone

Angular fragments of rock held together by a fine, sandy material

Breccia

Formed from the skeletons of micro-organisms, chalk has a soft, powdery texture

Chalk

IDENTIFYING MINERALS

No two minerals are the same, and many have a color or shape that will help identify them. Some form large crystals; others form bubbly masses or grow as crusts on rocks.

Vitreous, or glassy, luster

Quartz
One of the most common minerals, quartz occurs in many rocks, often in mineral veins with metal ores. Quartz crystals usually have six sides with a top shaped like a pyramid.

Gold
Gold is a precious metal and a rare native element. Usually found as yellow specks in rocks, it often grows with quartz in mineral veins. Occasionally gold forms large crystalline nuggets.

Prismatic beryl crystal

Beryl
Formed deep in the crust, beryl is found mainly in granites and pegmatites. Transparent beryl is a rare and valuable gemstone—emerald and aquamarine are the best-known varieties.

Pearly luster on crystals

Mass of tabular albite crystals

Albite
Usually white or colorless, albite is an important variety of feldspar, a rock-forming mineral, and is often found in granites, schists, and sandstones.

Cockscomb barite
Barite forms in many environments, from hot volcanic springs to mineral veins. Cockscomb barite is made up of rounded masses of soft, pearly crystals.

Sapphire crystals with tourmaline

Corundum
The pure form of corundum is colorless, but it comes in many colors—rubies and sapphires are two rare forms, mostly found in river gravels. Corundum is extremely hard.

Flat-topped, bright yellow crystal

Calcite
The main mineral in limestone, which usually forms in a marine environment, calcite is also found in bone and shell, and makes stalactites and stalagmites.

Sulfur
A native element, sulfur crystallizes around hot springs and volcanic craters, as a powdery crust of small crystals or as large crystals. Pure crystals are always yellow and soft.

Orange halite crystals

Halite
Best known as rock salt, halite is one of the minerals called evaporites, which form when salty water evaporates. It is found in masses and as cubic crystals, around seas and lakes in dry climates.

Find out more

Rocks are all around you, on the ground and in walls, buildings, and sculptures. The best way to find out more about them is to collect them. Going on a trip or vacation can also provide a chance to find different rocks and discover new types of landscape. Here you will find suggestions for extensive museum collections and other good places to visit, as well as a list of useful websites.

Collecting pebbles
Pebble beaches, lakesides, and riverbanks are good places to look for specimens. See how many colors and types you can find. Always be careful near water.

Gathering information
Visit your local natural history or geological museum to see rocks and minerals, rare and common. Many museums also have displays on volcanoes, earthquakes, and rocks from space.

Earth L

Identifying specimens
You can take rock samples to some museums for help in identifying them. T Earth Lab at the Natural History Museu in London has 2,000 specimens of rocks minerals, and fossils, plus microscopes, qualified advisers, and an online data si

PLACES TO VISIT

The following are some of the best natural history museums in the United States.

- **AMERICAN MUSEUM OF NATURAL HISTORY, NEW YORK, NEW YORK**

- **NATIONAL MUSEUM OF NATURAL HISTORY, SMITHSONIAN INSTITUTION WASHINGTON, D.C.**

- **CALIFORNIA MINING AND MINERAL MUSEUM, MARIPOSA, CALIFORNIA**

- **THE FIELD MUSEUM CHICAGO, ILLINOIS**

Displaying your collection
Gently clean your rock samples with water and let them dry, then arrange them in empty matchboxes or small cardboard trays. For delicate items, line the trays with tissue paper. Put a small data card in the base of each tray, with the specimen's name, where you found it, and when.

Cardboard trays lined with tissue

Specimen labels

USEFUL WEBSITES

- A searchable guide to gemstones and minerals that offers photos, a glossary, and resources: **www.minerals.net**
- Find how rocks and minerals form and how to collect and identify rocks and minerals: **www.rocksforkids.com**
- The Minerology Database contains information on over 4,000 minerals, grouped by property: **www.webmineral.com**

Gemstones and jewelry

A good place to look for jewelry and other objects carved from rock is at a museum that features decorative arts, such as The Metropolitan Meseum of Art in New York.

Aztec jade necklace

The Grand Canyon

History in the rocks

The Grand Canyon, in Arizona, gives visitors a superb view of different layers of Earth's rocks. The canyon was carved out by the Colorado River over several million years. The rocks are mostly sandstones and limestones, and they contain bands of fossils from different geological periods. Going down the steep trails to the bottom is like traveling back in time.

Sculptures

Ancient Greeks and Romans used marble for fine statues and buildings. Look at statues closely to see if they are made from marble or another stone.

Marble statue of Pieta, St. Patrick's Cathedral, New York

Giant's steps

At the Giant's Causeway in Northern Ireland visitors can see hexagonal columns of rock up to 7 ft (2 m) tall. Legends says a giant built them as stepping-stones across the sea. In fact, they formed when basalt lava cooled and shrank.

Cave at Melissani, Cephalonia, Greece

Limestone caves and grottos

Limestone caves are good places to see stalactites. There are blue grottos on Mediterranean islands, such as Cephalonia and Malta. The Lascaux Caves in France have prehistoric cave paintings.

Glossary

ABRASION Erosion caused by water, wind, or ice laden with sediments, and scraping or rubbing against the surface of rocks.

ACICULAR Having a needlelike form.

ALLOY A metallic material, such as brass, bronze, or steel, that is a mixture of two types of metal.

CABOCHON A gemstone cut in which the stone has a smooth, domed upper surface without any facets.

CARAT The standard measure of weight for precious stones. One metric carat equals 0.2 g (0.007oz). Also used to describe the purity of gold; pure gold is 24 carat.

CLEAVAGE The way a crystal splits apart along certain well-defined planes according to its internal structure.

CORE The area of iron and nickel that makes up the center of the Earth. It is about 850 miles (1,370 km) in diameter.

CRUST The thin outer layer of the Earth. It varies in thickness between 4 and 43 miles (7 and 70 km).

Group of natural crystals

CRYSTAL A naturally occurring solid with a regular internal structure and smooth external faces.

DENDRITIC Having a branchlike form.

DEPOSIT A buildup of sediments.

ELEMENT One of the basic substances from which all matter is made. An element cannot be broken down into a simpler substance.

EROSION The wearing away of rocks on the Earth's surface by gravity, wind, water, and ice.

Ground worn away by erosion

EVAPORITE Mineral or rock formed as a result of salt or spring water evaporating.

EXTRUSIVE ROCK Formed when magma erupts as lava, which cools at the surface.

FACE A surface of a crystal.

FACET One side of a cut gemstone.

FIRE In gemstones, dispersed light. A gem with strong fire, like a diamond, is very bright.

FOSSIL The remains or traces of plants or animals preserved in Earth's crust, in rock, amber, permafrost, or tar.

GALVANIZATION A process that adds zince to other metals or alloys to prevent them from rusting.

GEMSTONE Naturally occurring minerals, usually in crystal form, that are valued for beauty, rarity, and hardness.

GEOLOGIST A person who studies rocks and minerals to find out the structure of Earth's crust and how it formed.

Ammonite fossil

HABIT The shape and general appearance of a crystal or group of crystals.

INTRUSIVE ROCKS Igneous rocks that solidify within Earth's crust and only appear at the surface once the rocks lying on top of them have eroded away.

IRIDESCENCE A rainbowlike play of colors on the surface of a mineral, similar to that of a film of oil on water.

KARST SCENERY The broken rock formations of some limestone plateaus.

LAPIDARY A professional gem cutter.

LAVA Red-hot, molten rock (magma) from deep within the Earth that erupts on to the surface in volcanoes and other vents.

LUSTER The way in which a mineral shines. It is affected by how light is reflected from the surface of the mineral.

MAGMA Molten rock below the Earth's surface.

MANTLE The layer between Earth's core and crust. It is 1,800 miles (2,900 km) thick.

MASSIVE A term used to describe a mineral that has no definite shape.

MATRIX A mass of small grains surrounding large grains in a sedimentary rock.

METAMORPHOSE To undergo a change of structure. In rocks, this is usually caused by the action of heat or pressure.

METEORITE An object from space, such as a rock, that survives its passage through the atmosphere to reach Earth.

MINERAL A naturally occurring, inorganic solid with certain definite characteristics, such as crystal structure and chemical composition.

MINERAL VEIN A crack in rock filled by hot fluids' mineral deposits.

MOHS' SCALE A scale of hardness from 1 to 10 based on 10 minerals. Minerals of a higher number are able to scratch those of a lower number.

Diamond

Sapphire

Meteorite

MOLTEN Melted, made into a liquid by great heat, especially rocks.

NATIVE ELEMENT An element that occurs naturally in a free state and does not form part of a compound.

NODULE A rounded lump of mineral found in sedimentary rock.

OOLITH Small, rounded grains in limestones.

OPAQUE Material that does not let light pass through it.

OPTICAL PROPERTIES The various optical effects produced as light passes through minerals. This is one of the properties used to help identify minerals.

ORE A rock or mineral deposit that is rich enough in metal or gemstone for it to be worth extracting.

OUTCROP The area that one type of rock covers on a geological map, including the parts covered by soil or buildings.

PALEONTOLOGIST A scientist who studies fossils.

PIGMENT A natural coloring material often used in paints and dyes. Many pigments were first made by crushing colored rocks and mixing the powders with animal fats.

POROUS Able to absorb water, air, or other fluids.

PORPHYRY An igneous rock containing fairly large crystals set into a finer matrix.

PRECIPITATION A chemical process during which a solid substance, such as lime, is deposited from a solution, such as lime-rich water.

Azurite, once ground into a prized blue pigment

PYROCLASTIC ROCK Pyroclastic means "fire-broken" and describes all the fragments of rock, pumice, and solid lava that may be exploded out of a volcano.

RESIN A sticky substance that comes from some plants and may harden to form amber, valued as a gem.

ROCK An aggregate of mineral particles.

Stalactites hanging from the roof of a cave

SEDIMENT Rock material of various sizes, ranging from boulders to silt, which is the product of weathering and erosion, as well as shell fragments and other organic material.

SMELTING The process of melting ore to extract the metal that it contains.

SPECIFIC GRAVITY A property defined by comparing the weight of a mineral with the weight of an equal volume of water.

STALACTITE A hanging spike made of calcium carbonate (lime) formed as dripping water precipitates lime from the roof of a cave. Over a long period of time, stony stalactites build up in size and may hang many feet from a cave roof.

STALAGMITE A stony spike standing on the base of a limestone cave. Stalagmites form where water has dripped from the roof of the cave or a stalactite above, slowly building up lime deposits.

STREAK The color produced when a mineral is crushed into a fine powder. The color of a streak is used to help identify minerals. It is often a better means of identification than the color of the mineral itself, since it is less variable.

STRIATIONS Parallel scratches, grooves, or lines on a crystal face that develop as the crystal grows.

SWALLOW HOLE A hollow in the ground, especially in limestone, where a surface stream disappears from sight and flows underground.

TRANSLUCENT Material that allows some light to pass through it, but is not clear.

TRANSPARENT Material that allows light to pass through it. It can be seen through.

TUMBLING The process of rolling rough mineral pieces in a tumbling machine with water and gradated sizes of grit until the pebbles are rounded and polished.

VEIN A deposit of foreign minerals within a rock fracture or a joint.

VESICLE A gas bubble or cavity in lava that is left as a hole after the lava has cooled and solidified.

Veins of calcite

VOLCANIC BOMB A blob of lava that is thrown out of a volcano and solidifies before hitting the ground.

VOLCANIC VENT The central passage in a volcano, or a narrow fissure in the ground or on the seafloor through which magma flows and erupts as lava.

WEATHERING The breaking down of rocks on the Earth's surface. This is mainly a chemical reaction, aided by the presence of water, but it may also be due to processes such as alternate freezing and thawing, or to mechanical weathering by sediment-laden wind or ice.

Index

Acknowledgments

Dorling Kindersley would like to thank:
Dr. Wendy Kirk of University College London; the staff of the British Museum (Natural History); Gavin Morgan, Nick Merryman, & Christine Jones at the Museum of London for their advice & invaluable help in providing specimens; Redland Brick Company & Jacobson Hirsch for the loan of equipment; Anne-marie Bulat for her work on the initial stages of the book; David Nixon for design assistance; Tim Hammond for editorial assistance; Fred Ford & Mike Pilley of Radius Graphics, and Ray Owen & Nick Madren for artwork.

For this relaunch edition, the publisher would also like to thank: Camilla Hallinan for text editing and Carron Brown for proofreading

The publisher would like to thank the following for their kind permission to reproduce their images:
a=above, b=bottom, c=center, f=far, l=left, m=middle, r=right, t=top

Airbus-image exm company: P. Masclet 56bl. **Ardea London Ltd.:** Francois Gohier 65t. **Didier Barrault / Robert Harding Picture Library:** 37mr. **Bridgeman Art Library / Bonhoms, London:** 55mr. **Paul Brierley:** 49b; 51m. **British Museum (Natural History):** 42m; 43. **N. A. Callow / Robert Harding Picture Library:** 13b. **Bruce Coleman Ltd:** Derek Croucher 69br; Jeff Foott 65bl; Natural Selection Inc 64br. **G. & P. Corrigan / Robert Harding Picture Library:** 23t. **GeoScience Features Picture Library:** 68tr. **Diamond information Centre:** 60m. **C. M. Dixon / Photoresources:** 11b; 14t; 15t; 19b; 32b. **Earth Satellite Corporation / Science Photo Library:** 7t. **Mary Evans Picture Library:** 6t; 8; 9m; 12b; 15b; 16tl; 19t; 25; 26b; 28b; 30bl; 31b; 32t; 34t, ml; 36t; 37t, bl; 39b; 40t; 41t; 44tr; 50tr, br; 56mr; 57m; 58tl, tr; 59tl, b; 62t, m. **Clive Friend / Woodmansterne Ltd.:** 15m, 36b. **Jon Gardey / Robert Harding Picture Library:** 40b. **Geoscience Features:** 18t. **Mike Gray / University College London:** 17; 20tr; 24tf. **Ian Griffiths / Robert Harding Picture Library:** 13t. **Robert Harding Picture Library:** 13m; 18br; 21; 22bl; 23m; 27t, b; 35t, b; 56t; 59m. **Brian Hawkes / Robert Harding Picture Library:** 12m. **Michael Holford:** 50tl, bl; 51t; 54t, mr; 55t, ml. **Glenn I. Huss:** 40m. **The Hutchinson Library:** 35m; 51b; 56ml. **INAH:** Michel Zabé 69tr. **Yoram Lehmann / Robert Harding Picture Library:** 37ml. **Kenneth Lucas / Planet Earth:** 39t. **Johnson Matthey:** 58bl. **Museum of London:** 28t; 32m; 61tl, br. **NASA:** 41br. **NASA/Robert Harding Picture Library:** 6–7, 7b. **NASA / Spectrum Color Library:** 11t. **National Coal Board:** 37br. **The Natural History Museum, London:** 68cl, 68cr, 71crb. **N.H.P.A.:** Kevin Schafer 64cl. **Walter Rawlings / Robert Harding Picture Library:** 26m; 33b. **John G. Ross/Robert Harding Picture Library:** 53. **K. Scholz / ZEFA:** 10b. **Nicholas Servian / Woodmansterne:** 34mr. **Silva:** 62crb. **A. Sorrell / Museum of London:** 29t. **Science Photo Library:** Charles D. Winters: jacket, b. **Spectrum Color Library:** 10m. **R. F. Symes:** 9tr. **A. C. Waltham / Robert Harding Picture Library:** 22br. **Werner Forman Archive:** 29b; 30br; 31tl, ml; 52t, b, 55b; 61m. **G. M. Wilkins / Robert Harding Picture Library:** 47. **Woodmansterne:** 58br. **ZEFA:** 16tr. **Zeiss:** 41bl. **Reproduced with the premission of the Controller of Her Majesty's Stationery Office, Crown copyright:** 54ml. **Illustrations:** Andrew Macdonald 6m, b; 14ml; 18bl; 22ml; 28mr; 30mr.

All other images © Dorling Kindersley. For further information, see: **www.dkimages.com**